the Magic Vine Quilt

Eleanor Burns

For my Mother, Erma Dora Drushel Knoechel

My mother has always loved flowers. Her happiest moments were spent in her garden planting or pulling weeds. Her prized treasure was her phlox that she dug from her grandmother's garden and transplanted to every home we lived in. Every summer, Mother gathered beautiful bouquets and delivered them to our neighbors.

Mother taught me to also love the flowers! Last spring while walking Tabatha and Peanut, I happened upon this beautiful field of California poppies… a gift from nature and my mother.

First Edition
April, 2007
Published by Quilt in a Day®, Inc.
1955 Diamond Street, San Marcos, CA 92078
©2007 by Eleanor A. Burns Family Trust

ISBN 1-891776-22-3

Art Director: Merritt Voigtlander
Production Artists: Marie Harper, Ann Huisman

Table of Contents

Introduction

I have found a kindred soul mate in Florence LaGanke Harris, the original designer of the Magic Vine flower blocks. Even though we lived a short distance apart in the late 60's and 70's, we never met. Florence lived in Cleveland, Ohio, as Foods Editor for the Cleveland Press Newspaper. At the same time, I lived in Pittsburgh, Pennsylvania, teaching special education. It's quilts that brought us together years later.

As a quilt pattern designer, Florence wrote a syndicated nationwide newspaper column under the title of the "Nancy Page Quilt Club," starting in the early 1930's and ran the column for seventeen years. My path followed with the Quilt in a Day "Block Party", started in 1984.

Each week, Florence printed one pattern from a quilt and gave her readers a week to complete the block. A fascinating fictional serial story about Nancy and her friends typical of the times ran along with the pattern.

My students get a whole month to finish their block, and we have just as much fun at our monthly gatherings as Nancy and her friends! I know, because I've read about Nancy's gatherings through my collection of Florence's newspaper clippings, including Grandmother's Garden, and now Magic Vine.

Having published over eighty books, I can certainly identify with Florence's weekly deadlines of getting the pattern to press on time! In one of her columns, a neighbor of Nancy asked what other flowers there were going to be in the quilt. Nancy answered, "I told her we never knew from week to week just what the next pattern would be. I told her that made the quilt so much more exciting." How similar our lives ran together! I answer that way, too, because I haven't figured it out yet!

We share so many other things as well. Florence established a Quilt Clinic where women came to learn how to make quilts and exhibit the quilts they had made. Attendance was anywhere from 40 to 1000. Her clinic sounds just like the event Quilt in a Day holds every April in Paducah, Kentucky with 3000 enthusiastic quilters attending energetic quilt shows in a circus tent.

Florence LaGanke Harris

All twenty-two flower patterns are included in *Magic Vine Quilt* as originally designed by Nancy with some simplification. Blocks are 1" larger than original size. I had fun designing a bright, quaint fabric line to go with the Magic Vine flowers. Coincidentally, the line is called "Magic Vine," manufactured by Benartex!

Sit back, relax with a cup of tea, and enjoy reading the old newspaper clippings from Florence and Nancy. Then dig into your own stash of flower fabrics, or run out and buy all new fabrics. Plant the seeds of creativity in your own Magic Vine Quilt.

Eleanor Burns

*Mr. Bonfils,
the publisher of The
Post in 1930, asked women
who delight in handwork to clip the
Nancy Page patterns for future reference. I
extend a grateful thank you to Stella Von De Wynchel
of Ontario, Canada for sharing her old patterns.*

Antique Magic Vine Quilt

The unknown maker of this quilt closely followed the Nancy Page newspaper series and made forty-four flowers as suggested. Each vine has eleven flowers, but the first and third vines use the same flowers, and the second and fourth repeat. Notice how the quilter made dark vines and leaves with medium overlapping leaves in the first and third vines, and reversed the greens in the second and fourth rows.

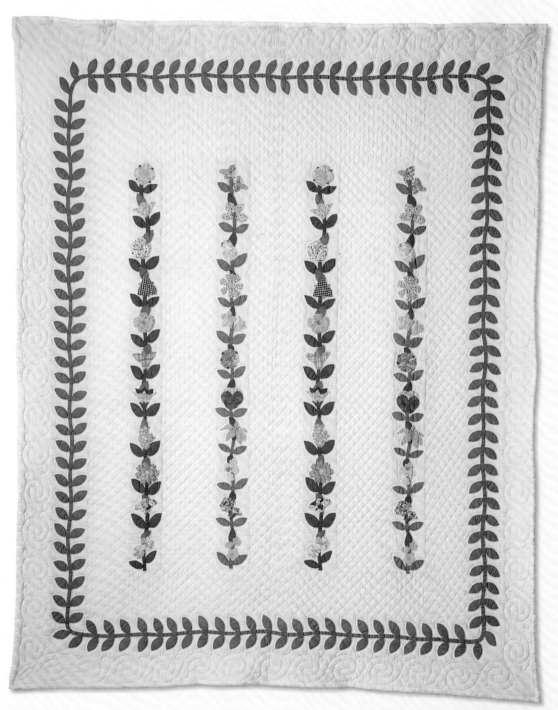

Quilt owned by Deborah Dilly, LaSalle, CO
Hand Quilted by Tina Kirk, Edwardsville, IL

82" x 104"

Follow along with Nancy Page as she explains the quilt and suggests several colors for your flowers.

New Series for Those Who Enjoy Handwork

but it could be made into such a lovely one to dream under, and would give each of us such a splendid chance to express our taste and individuality in selecting colors for it. We could put all sorts of flowers on it and if it were a Magic Vine, there is no reason why flowers of hill and dale couldn't spring from a common stem.

So that is how this pet quilt of mine came to be, and I do hope that you will like it."

The neighborhood club members gathered early at Nancy's home. She had Lois, who really had suggested the idea for the new quilt, hold up a large drawing of the quilt as it would look when finished.

At each club meeting we will make one block of the vine and join it to its neighbor. There are four vines down the center part of the quilt. There are 44 flowers on these vines all told. Each vine has 11. But the first and third vine use the same flowers and the second and fourth repeat. That means we have 22 flower patterns to work out.

Then we need a pattern for the border vine and its leaves. But we come to that soon enough.

Nancy Page writes us that she got the idea for the quilt from Jack and his magic bean vine and the fact that her own little daughter was growing just like that vine and the flowers.

"Why not make a Magic Vine quilt to dream under?" she wondered.

"You remember how quickly the vine of fairy tale fame grew and what wonders it enabled Jack to perform? Well, I began to wonder why not have a Magic Vine quilt the kind that never really was, you know,

Planning Your Quilt

Selecting Your Style

Depending on the selection of your block layout, background, and fabrics for your flowers, different looks are created. Select from these three layouts, or use a combination and create your own style.

Blocks Set in Straight Vertical Rows

This is the original Nancy Page layout with flowers sewn on 7½" Background squares, and then sewn together in straight vertical rows. Vines on the blocks are connected from one to the next with an overlapping leaf. Vertical rows are set together with matching Background fabric.

To bring color from the flowers into the outside edge, you can piece a colorful rainbow border and binding for a scallop or wave edge.

Information and yardage charts for blocks set straight in vertical rows begin on page 16.

37" x 48"

Blocks Set on Point with Solid Squares

This setting, a variation from the original straight setting, is the easiest. Flowers are sewn to 7½" Background squares on point, and are then set together with solid squares the same size.

In this setting, flower stems curve to the left or right, so overlapping leaves are not necessary. Select solid squares in fabric the same as the Background, or a fabric complimentary to flower colors.

Blocks are sewn together on the diagonal with side and corner triangles. In this example, flowers are accented with a rickrack, and a wave outside edge. Quilts also can be finished with a rainbow border and binding.

Information and yardage charts for blocks set on point with solid squares begin on page 20.

39" x 49"

Blocks Set on Point with Lattice

This setting is also a variation from the original. Flowers are sewn to 7½" Background squares on point. Stems curve to the left or right, so overlapping leaves are not necessary. Blocks are then set together with side and corner triangles in straight rows. In this layout, striped lattice in one or two widths can be used to set straight rows together. Background the same as the flower blocks can also be used. For additional color, piece a rainbow border and straight edge binding or bias binding for a scallop or wave edge.

Information and yardage charts for blocks set on point with lattice begin on page 24.

45" x 58"

Selecting Your Fabrics

Background Choices

Select fabrics with a high thread count. Beware of thin fabric because it puckers excessively when appliquéing flowers.

For an old fashioned look, select natural, white, or soft pastel in a good quality fabric. Do not select a medium background because flowers will not stand out.

For a contemporary look, select a soft colored batik, light tone on tone, or a mottled black.

Each yardage chart lists how much fabric is needed for your size quilt.

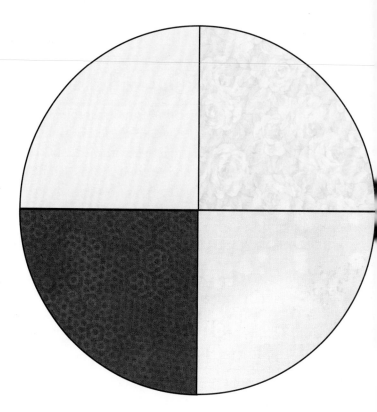

Contemporary Flower and Leaf Colors

Look for fabrics with subtle textures and slight variations in hue, such as batiks or Fossil Ferns. Choose mottled fabrics with areas of light and dark to show shading and dimension. Large scale florals can be fussy cut into petals, centers, and leaves. For zing, throw in a polka dot, a stripe, or a bold pattern.

Because only small pieces are needed for the flowers, it's fun to have a large variety of fabrics. Purchase ⅛ or ¼ yard fat quarters and combine them with what's in your stash.

Separate your stash into color families, mixing two or three related fabrics for each flower. Separate violets into red-violets, and blue-violets. Separate reds from light pinks to deep magenta.

Nancy warned the club members about the necessity of choosing only color fast material. This is still good current advice. Spray your fabrics with water to make certain they don't bleed. For extra caution, prewash fabrics with Synthrapol or Dye Magnet.

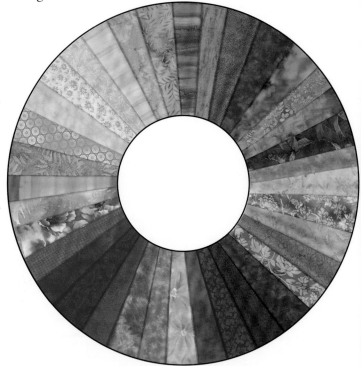

Select three different values of yellow, orange, red to pink, purple, and blue. Vary the scale and texture as well.

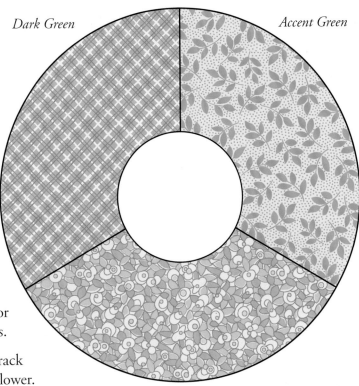

Old Fashioned Leaf Colors

In the original quilt, Nancy Page suggested using a medium green and a dark green for stems and leaves, plus a third green for accent. In each row of flowers, the pair of leaves and stems were one value, and if used, the overlapping leaf was the opposite value. These two green combinations switch back and forth.

If you choose to remain "pure" to the original quilt, purchase three different greens. Or, if you choose to be original, purchase one green for stems, and a variety of textured greens for leaves.

As a substitute for green fabric stems, wide rickrack can be used. Purchase 6" of rickrack for every flower.

Old Fashioned Flower Colors

Select three fabrics each in different values of yellow, orange, pink, purple, blue, and red. Vary the scale and texture as well.

In addition, purchase thread slightly darker than the colors of flowers or contrasting thread. If you intend to hand stitch centers, purchase embroidery floss or #5 and #8 pearl cotton in a color selection of your choice. Typical colors to select include two colors of yellow, brown, black, purple, green, and pink.

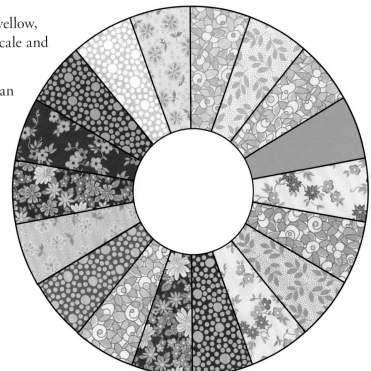

These fabrics are part of the Magic Vine line from Benartex, designed by Eleanor Burns with the help of Patricia Knoechel.

Selecting Your Flower Making Technique

Two basic methods are described.
- Quick Turn Appliqué
- Raw Edge Appliqué

Detailed instructions for **Quick Turn Appliqué** begin on page 36.
Raw Edge Appliqué begins on page 58.

Quick Turn Appliqué

Quick Turn Appliqué is the more time consuming of the two methods. It is more durable and relaxing if you enjoy handwork. Quilts can be used and washed without worry of outside edges fraying.

The special product used in this method is **light weight, non-woven fusible interfacing**. It's pliable, more like fabric than paper, and comes in 22" width. It has a smooth side, and a textured fusible side. Pellon brand is recommended and does not require preshrinking. Test several brands to find your favorite. Since home iron temperatures vary, also test the process to determine which setting is the best for your iron.

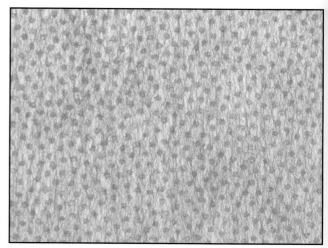

Light weight, non-woven fusible interfacing has a smooth side, and a textured fusible side.

Flower patterns are drawn on the smooth side of fusible interfacing. Fabric for flowers and fusible interfacing are then stitched together, and quick turned so that raw edges are turned inside. Turned flowers are then fused to Background squares and outside edges are stitched down.

Light dimension can be added to largest applique pieces by "stuffing" or padding them with thin 100% cotton batting. Since pieces are permanently pressed after being "stuffed," cotton batting must be used as polyester will melt and compress.

When flower fabric and interfacing are stitched together and turned, raw edges are turned inside. Flowers can also be "stuffed" for extra dimension.

Quick Turn flowers can be finished by hand or machine. In this example, quick turned edges were hand appliquéd in place and decorative hand stitching was added to the center. Beads or crystals can also be added, but not until after quilting is compeled.

In this Straight Set example, the Arrowhead is old fashioned looking in a 1930's reproduction print sewn to a natural Background. Dark green was used on the stem and leaves, and medium green for the overlapping leaf. A pink flower was centered, or "fussy cut", on the stamens.

Outside edges can also be hand or machine finished with a blanket stitch.

Edges of the False Beech Drop were finished by hand.

Edges of the Milkwort were finished by machine.

13

Raw Edge Appliqué

Raw Edge Appliqué is the quicker of the two methods, with outside raw edges finished by machine. It's possibly not as durable as Quick Turn Appliqué. However, it's perfect for quilts that will not be laundered often.

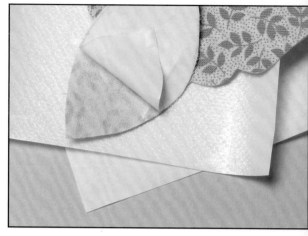

The special product used in this method is **paper backed fusible web.** Two recommended brands are Steam-A-Seam 2® and Wonder Under®. Try several to find your favorite. Keep in mind that the web shouldn't be so heavy that your sewing machine needle can not penetrate. The product can also get old and will refuse to bond two fabrics together.

Fusible web has a dull paper side, and a shiny fusible side.

Fusible web has a dull paper side and a shiny fusible side. It's usually 12" to 17" wide. Yardage charts are based on a 17"width. Flower patterns are drawn on the paper side. The opposite webbed side is fused to the wrong side of the flower fabric. Pieces are cut out with sharp scissors. The paper is peeled away, and flowers are then fused in place on Background fabric.

The Straight Set Pansy was made using contemporary batik fabric in three different values of purple with an added touch of yellow. A soft green Background sets off the brilliant purple colors and deeper textured greens for stems and leaves.

The web was light enough that a hand sewing needle was used to stitch several Crystals in the center. Outside edges were satin stitched.

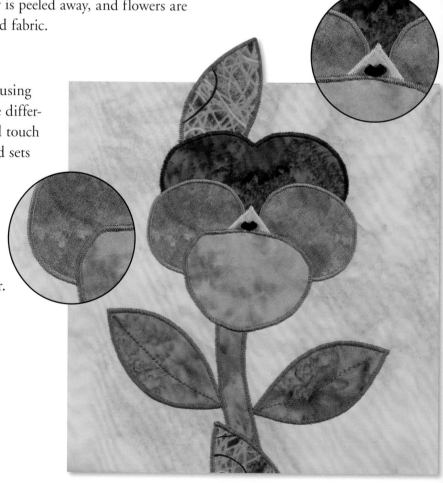

Outside edges of the Pansy were machine satin stitched.

Another machine stitch that can be used is the blanket stitch.

Outside edges can also be finished with a straight stitch, ⅛" from raw edges.

Place **tear-away stabilizer** under blocks when outside edges ripple with stitching. Cut stabilizers at 7½" to completely cover back sides of Background squares. If you cut the stabilizer smaller, chances are good it won't be under the areas you need stitched!

Many products are available, and you should test several to find your favorite. Make sure it can be easily torn away from the backside after stitching. Substitutes include tissue paper sold by the roll and round coffee filters.

Cut stabilizer at 7½" to completely cover back sides of Background squares.

Yardage Charts
Blocks Set Straight in Vertical Rows

To get the effect of a climbing vine, blocks are arranged with Stems alternating back and forth, changing direction with each block. If you change your arrangement of Flowers, you may need to change the direction of your Stems.

The Wallhanging quilt needs eight blocks. Photocopy the little blocks on next page, select the ones you want to make, and arrange them so similar colors, sizes, and shapes of Flowers are equally spaced.

The Lap needs twenty-one Flowers blocks. Use the back cover quilt as your guide for setting blocks in rows, and selecting greens for Stems and Leaves.

For the Twin, Full/Queen and King quilts, make duplicate Flowers in the order given, and sew them together in rows. First, third, and fifth rows of Flowers are the same, and second and fourth rows are the same. The Full/Queen and King quilts are exceptionally long. If desired, leave off the top outside border to reduce its length. Refer to illustrations on pages 160 to 161.

Rows One, Three, and Five
Pairs of Leaves and Stems are dark green. The Overlapping Leaf is medium green.

Rows Two and Four
Pairs of Leaves and Stems are medium green. The Overlapping Leaf is dark green.

Overlapping Leaf
Notice that the top block in each row does not have an Overlapping Leaf at the very top, but has an Overlapping Leaf between it and the second block. The last block in each row has an Overlapping Leaf only at the top, and not at the bottom.

Pieced by Patricia Knoechel
Quilted by Amie Potter
Queen size with Four Rows

	Rows One, Three and Five	Rows Two and Four	
	Evening Primrose Page 68	Shooting Star Page 112	
	Arrowhead Page 72	Poppy Page 116	
	Phlox Page 76	Tulip Page 120	
Wallhanging Make any four blocks for Row One and any four blocks for Row Two.	Trillium Page 80 / Wallhanging	Cosmos Page 124	
	Blue Eyed Grass Page 84	Bluebell Page 128	
	Milkwort Page 88	Zinnia Page 132	
Lap Make seven blocks for Rows One and Three and seven blocks for Row Two. Follow the photograph on the left for twenty-one different Flowers.	Downy Gentian Page 92 / Lap	Pansy Page 136	
	False Beech Drop Page 96	Tiger Lily Page 140	
Twin Make three rows with ten blocks in each row. Rows One and Three are the same. Row Two has ten different Flowers.	Bouncing Bet Page 100	Forget Me Not Page 144	
Full/Queen Make four rows with eleven blocks in each row. Rows One and Three are the same. Rows Two and Four are the same.	Morning Glory Page 104 / Twin	Nasturtium Page 148	
King Make five rows with eleven blocks in each row. Rows One, Three and Five are the same. Rows Two and Four are the same.	Wild Rose Page 108 / Full/Queen / King	Buttercup Page 152	

You have permission to photocopy this page.

17

Yardage Chart for Blocks Set Straight in Vertical Rows

	Wallhanging 35" x 46" 8 Flower Blocks Two Rows of Four Each	Lap 45" x 66" 21 Flower Blocks Three Rows of Seven Each
Flower Colors Select colors based on Flower choices.	Two to Three fat eighths of each color Yellow, pink, blue, purple, orange, red	Two to Three fat quarters of each color Yellow, pink, blue, purple, orange, red
Optional If you plan to make a Rainbow Border and/or Rainbow Bias Binding, cut these total pieces before cutting flowers.	Rainbow Border (20) 2" x 8" pieces Bias Binding (19) 2¼" x 13" bias strips	Rainbow Border (28) 2" x 8" pieces Bias Binding (14) 2¼" x 22" bias strips
Stems and Leaves Dark Green and Medium Green	½ yd of each Cut from each (1) 16" x 20" piece for Stems (1) 3½" x 20" for Leaves	½ yd of each Cut from each (1) 16" x 20" piece for Stems (4) 3½" x 20" for Leaves
Accent Green	⅛ yd	⅛ yd
Optional Vine and Leaves for Border	¾ yd	1 yd
Quick Turn Appliqué Non-woven Fusible Interfacing Based on 22" width	1 yd (2) 3½" x 20" strips for Leaves Remainder for Flowers	2 yds (8) 3½" x 20" strips for Leaves Remainder for Flowers
100% Cotton Batting	⅛ yd	⅛ yd
Or Raw Edge Appliqué Paper backed fusible web Based on 17" width	2 yds (2) 16" x 20" pieces for Stems (2) 3½" x 20" strips for Leaves Remainder for Flowers	3 yds (2) 16" x 20" pieces for Stems (8) 3½" x 20" strips for Leaves Remainder for Flowers
Optional Tear Away Stabilizer Cut according to your product.	(8) 7½" squares	(21) 7½" squares
Background	1¾ yds	3¼ yds
Blocks	(2) 7½" strips cut into (8) 7½" squares for Blocks	(5) 7½" strips cut into (21) 7½" squares
Lattice and Border	(5) 3½" strips for Lattice	(2) 3½" strips Top and Bottom
Instructions are given for cutting Background strips lengthwise so there are no seams. If you prefer, cut strips selvage to selvage and piece them together.	(4) 6½" strips for Border	(1) 60" lengthwise strip cut into (4) 3½" strips for Lattice (4) 6½" strips for Border
Scallop or Wave Binding	½ yd (1) 16" strip cut into (11) 2¼" bias strips	1 yd (2) 16" strips cut into (14) 2¼" bias strips
Or Straight Binding	½ yd (5) 3" strips	⅔ yd (7) 3" strips
Backing	1¾ yds	3 yds Cut into two equal parts
Batting	44" x 55"	54" x 74"

Yardage Chart for Blocks Set Straight in Vertical Rows

Twin 65" x 100" 30 Flower Blocks Three Rows of Ten Each	Full/Queen 92" x 110" 44 Flower Blocks Four Rows of Eleven Each	King 105" x 112" 55 Flower Blocks Five Rows of Eleven Each
Two to Three fat quarters of each color Yellow, pink, blue, purple, orange, red	Two to Three fat quarters of each color Yellow, pink, blue, purple, orange, red	Two to Three fat quarters of each color Yellow, pink, blue, purple, orange, red
Rainbow Border (34) 2" x 8" pieces Bias Binding (21) 2¼" x 22" bias strips	Rainbow Border (42) 2" x 8" pieces Bias Binding (25) 2¼" x 22" bias strips	Rainbow Border (44) 2" x 8" pieces Bias Binding (26) 2¼" x 22" bias strips
⅔ yd of each Cut from each (1) 16" x 20" piece for Stems (6) 3½" x 20" for Leaves	¾ yd of each Cut from each (1) 16" x 20" piece for Stems (8) 3½" x 20" for Leaves	1 yd of each Cut from each (1) 16" x 20" piece for Stems (10) 3½" x 20" for Leaves
⅛ yd	⅛ yd	⅛ yd
1⅓ yds	1½ yds	1½ yds
3 yds (12) 3½" x 20" strips for Leaves Remainder for Flowers	4¼ yds (16) 3½" x 20" strips for Leaves Remainder for Flowers	5¼ yds (20) 3½" x 20" strips for Leaves Remainder for Flowers
¼ yd	¼ yd	¼ yd
4 yds (2) 16" x 20" pieces for Stems (12) 3½" x 20" strips for Leaves Remainder for Flowers	5¼ yds (2) 16" x 20" pieces for Stems (16) 3½" x 20" strips for Leaves Remainder for Flowers	6 yds (2) 16" x 20" pieces for Stems (20) 3½" x 20" strips for Leaves Remainder for Flowers
(30) 7½" squares	(44) 7½" squares	(55) 7½" squares
6½ yds (6) 7½" strips cut into (30) 7½" squares (2) 3½" strips for Top and Bottom (1) 72" lengthwise strip cut into (2) 3½" strips for Outside Lattice (2) 7½" strips for Lattice (1) 13" strip for Border (1) 82" lengthwise strip cut into (3) 13" strips for Border	9½ yds (9) 7½" strips cut into (44) 7½" squares (1) 80" lengthwise strip cut into (5) 7½" strips for Lattice (1) 85" lengthwise strip cut into (2) 15" strips for Border (1) 95" lengthwise strip cut into (2) 15" strips for Border (2) 2" strips for Top and Bottom Lattice	10¼ yds (11) 7½" strips cut into (55) 7½" squares (1) 80" lengthwise strip cut into (5) 7½" strips for Lattice (1) 85" lengthwise strip cut into (1) 7½" strip for Lattice (2) 15" strips for Border (1) 110" lengthwise strip cut into (2) 15" strips Top and Bottom Borders (2) 3½" strips Top and Bottom Lattice
1½ yds (3) 16" strips cut into (21) 2¼" bias strips	1½ yds (3) 16" strips cut into (25) 2¼" bias strips	1½ yds (3) 16" strips cut into (26) 2¼" bias strips
1 yd (9) 3" strips	1 yd (11) 3" strips	1 yd (11) 3" strips
6¼ yds Cut into two equal parts 76" x 111"	8½ yds Cut into three equal parts 98" x 118"	10 yds Cut into three equal parts 113" x 118"

Blocks Set On Point with Solid Squares

Flowers are set on point with curve of Stems alternating between blocks. Stems can be alternated or turned at random. Each Flower also has a pair of leaves **connected to the Stem**. Overlapping Leaves are not necessary, but can be used with smaller Flowers.

Solid squares and Border can be from the same fabric, or different.
If you choose, add embellishments of rickrack or a folded border. Outside edges of quilts can be finished with waves or scallops.

For larger quilt sizes, duplicates of Flowers need to be made. Study quilt layouts on pages 166 and 167 to plan Flower and Stem placement.

Pieced by Eleanor Burns
Quilted by Amie Potter
40" x 50"

In this lap quilt, Stems on Flowers are alternating consistently. Country rickrack frames the blocks, and outside edges are finished with Waves.

Solid square fabric was selected first for this wallhanging. Flower colors were then pulled. Stems on Flowers were set at random, giving them a frivolous appearance. A bright Folded Border and bias cut Border add charm.

Pieced by Beverly Burris
Quilted by Carol Selepec
34" x 34"

Photocopy the little blocks, select the ones you want to make, and arrange them so similar colors, sizes, and shapes of Flowers are equally spaced. Consistently alternate your Stems, or set them at random.

Rows One and Four   Rows Two and Five   Rows Three and Six

Wallhanging
Make any nine Flower blocks for three rows of three Flowers each.

Lap
Make any twelve Flower blocks for three rows of four Flowers each.

Twin
Make four rows with seven blocks in each row. Make twenty-one blocks for three rows, and repeat one of those rows for fourth row, or make Rows One and Three the same, and Rows Two and Four the same.

Full/Queen
Make six rows with seven blocks in each row. Rows One and Four are the same. Rows Two and Five are the same. Rows Three and Six are the same.

King
Make six rows with seven blocks in each row. Rows One, Four, and Seven are the same. Rows Two and Five are the same. Rows Three and Six are the same.

Twenty-one blocks are used for Twin through King. Make the twenty-second block for your label, so all flowers are included in your quilt.

You have permission to photocopy this page.

Yardage Chart for Blocks Set On Point with Solid Squares

	Wallhanging 37" x 37" 9 Flower Blocks Three Rows of Four Each	Lap 40" x 49" 12 Flower Blocks Three Rows of Four Each
Flower Colors Select colors based on Flower choices.	Two or Three fat eighths of each color Yellow, pink, blue, purple, orange, red	Two or Three fat quarters of each color Yellow, pink, blue, purple, orange, red
Optional If you plan to make a Rainbow Border and/or Rainbow Bias Binding, cut these total pieces before cutting flowers.	Rainbow Border (20) 2" x 8" pieces Bias Binding (16) 2¼" x 13" bias strips	Rainbow Border (22) 2" x 8" pieces Bias Binding (11) 2¼" x 22" bias strips

Stems and Leaves
    Dark Green and Medium Green
	½ yd of each Cut from each
	    (1) 16" x 20" piece for Stems
	    (1) 3½" x 20" for Leaves
		½ yd of each Cut from each
		    (1) 16" x 20" piece for Stems
		    (2) 3½" x 20" for Leaves

Accent Green	⅛ yd	⅛ yd
Optional Vine and Leaves for Border	¾ yd	1 yd

Quick Turn Appliqué
    Non-woven Fusible Interfacing
    Based on 22" Width
	⅔ yd
	    (2) 3½" x 20" strips for Leaves
	    Remainder for Flowers
		1 yd
		    (4) 3½" x 20" strips for Leaves
		    Remainder for Flowers

100% Cotton Batting	⅛ yd	⅛ yd

Or Raw Edge Appliqué
    Paper Backed Fusible Web
    Based on 17" Width
	2 yds
	    (2) 16" x 20" pieces for Stems
	    (2) 3½" x 20" strips for Leaves
	    Remainder for Flowers
		2¼ yds
		    (2) 16" x 20" pieces for Stems
		    (4) 3½" x 20" strips for Leaves
		    Remainder for Flowers

Optional Tear Away Stabilizer Cut according to your product.	(9) 7½" squares	(12) 7½" squares

Background	¾ yd
	    (2) 7½" strips cut into
	        (9) 7½" squares for Blocks
	    (4) 2" strips for First Border
		1 yd
		    (3) 7½" strips cut into
		        (12) 7½" squares for Blocks
		    (4) 2" strips for First Border

Optional Folded Border	¼ yd
	    (4) 1¼" strips
		¼ yd
		    (4) 1¼" strips

Setting Squares and Triangles	⅔ yd
	    Cut later
		1 yd
		    Cut later

Second Border	⅔ yd
	    (4) 5" strips
		¾ yd
		    (5) 5" strips

Scallop or Wave Binding
    One Fabric
	½ yd
	    (1) 16" strip cut into
	        (9) 2¼" bias strips
		½ yd
		    (1) 16" strip cut into
		        (11) 2¼" bias strips

Or Straight Binding
    One Fabric
	½ yd
	    (4) 3" strips
		½ yd
		    (5) 3" strips

Backing	1¼ yds	2⅔ yds Cut into two equal parts
Batting	44" x 55"	48" x 56"

Yardage Chart for Blocks Set On Point with Solid Squares

Twin 68" x 96" 28 Flower Blocks Four Rows of Seven Each	Full/Queen 90" x 100" 42 Flower Blocks Six Rows of Seven Each	King 100" x 100" 49 Flower Blocks Seven Rows of Seven Each
Two or Three fat quarters of each color Yellow, pink, blue, purple, orange, red	Two or Three fat quarters of each color Yellow, pink, blue, purple, orange, red	Two or Three fat quarters of each color Yellow, pink, blue, purple, orange, red
Rainbow Border (28) 2" x 8" pieces Bias Binding (20) 2¼" x 22" bias strips	Rainbow Border (38) 2" x 8" pieces Bias Binding (23) 2¼" x 22" bias strips	Rainbow Border (40) 2" x 8" pieces Bias Binding (24) 2¼" x 22" bias strips

½ yd of each Cut from each
    (1) 16" x 20" piece for Stems
    (3) 3½" x 20" for Leaves
	⅔ yd of each Cut from each
	    (1) 16" x 20" piece for Stems
	    (5) 3½" x 20" for Leaves
		1 yd of each Cut from each
		    (1) 16" x 20" piece for Stems
		    (5) 3½" x 20" for Leaves

⅛ yd	⅛ yd	⅛ yd
1⅓ yds	1½ yds	1½ yds

2¼ yds
    (6) 3½" x 20" strips for Leaves
    Remainder for Flowers
	3½ yds
	    (10) 3½" x 20" strips for Leaves
	    Remainder for Flowers
		4 yds
		    (10) 3½" x 20" strips for Leaves
		    Remainder for Flowers

¼ yd	¼ yd	¼ yd

3¼ yds
    (2) 16" x 20" pieces for Stems
    (6) 3½" x 20" strips for Leaves
    Remainder for Flowers
	4½ yds
	    (2) 16" x 20" pieces for Stems
	    (10) 3½" x 20" strips for Leaves
	    Remainder for Flowers
		5 yds
		    (2) 16" x 20" pieces for Stems
		    (10) 3½" x 20" strips for Leaves
		    Remainder for Flowers

(28) 7½" squares	(42) 7½" squares	(49) 7½" squares

2 yds
    (6) 7½" strips cut into
        (28) 7½" squares for Blocks
    (6) 3½" strips for First Border
	2¾ yds
	    (9) 7½" strips cut into
	        (42) 7½" squares for Blocks
	    (7) 3½" strips for First Border
		3¼ yds
		    (10) 7½" strips cut into
		        (49) 7½" squares for Blocks
		    (8) 3½" strips for First Border

¼ yd (6) 1¼" strips	⅓ yd (7) 1¼" strips	⅓ yd (8) 1¼" strips

1¾ yds
    Cut later
	2⅛ yds
	    Cut later
		2⅝ yds
		    Cut later

3¾ yds
    (9) 14" strips
	4¾ yds
	    (10) 15" strips
		4¾ yds
		    (10) 15" strips

1 yd
    (2) 16" strips cut into
        (20) 2¼" bias strips
	1½ yds
	    (3) 16" strips cut into
	        (23) 2¼" bias strips
		1½ yds
		    (3) 16" strips cut into
		        (24) 2¼" bias strips

1 yd
    (9) 3" strips
	1 yd
	    (11) 3" strips
		1 yd
		    (11) 3" strips

6 yds Cut into two equal parts	8 yds Cut into three equal parts	9½ yds Cut into three equal parts
76" x 104"	98" x 108"	106" x 106"

Blocks Set On Point with Lattice

Flowers are set on point with curves of Stems alternating between blocks. Stems can consistently or randomly alternate. Each Flower has a pair of Leaves connected to the Stem. Block Background, Setting Squares, and Lattice can be from the same fabric, or different. Finish outside edges with waves or scallops.

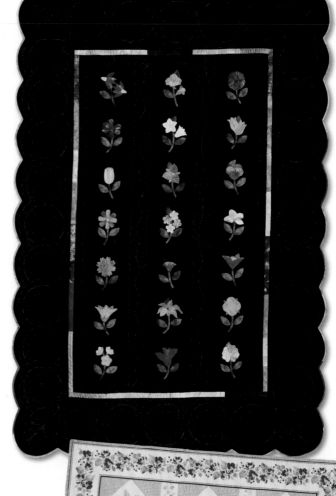

Pieced by Beverly Burris
Quilted by Carol Selepec
67" x 97"

A stripe fabric with two different widths approximately 3½" and 5½" is perfect for this setting. Use narrow stripe for Inside Lattice, and wide stripe for Outside Lattice. Check your size yardage chart for how many stripes of each are needed. Cut stripes on vertical lines, allowing for ¼" seam allowance.

Pieced by Teresa Varnes
Quilted by Janna Mitchell
45" x 58"

Photocopy little blocks, select the ones you want to make, and arrange them so similar colors, sizes, and shapes of Flowers are equally spaced. Consistently alternate Stems, or set them at random. For larger sizes, duplicate Flowers need to be made. Follow layouts on pages 176 and 177, or create your own layout.

Rows One and Four

Rows Two and Five

Rows Three and Six

You have permission to photocopy this page.

Wallhanging
Make any six Flowers for two rows of three Flowers each.

Lap
Make any fifteen Flowers for three rows of five Flowers each.

Twin
Make twenty-one Flowers for three rows of seven Flowers each. Make one each of twenty-two Flowers, and use the extra one for the label on the back.

Full/Queen
Make thirty-five Flowers for five rows of seven Flowers each. Rows One and Four are the same; Rows Two and Five are the same.

King
Make forty-two Flowers for six rows of seven Flowers each. Rows One and Four are the same; Rows Two and Five are the same; Rows Three and Six are the same.

Yardage Chart for Blocks Set On Point with Lattice

	Wallhanging 40" x 49" 6 Flower Blocks Two Rows of Three Each	Lap 55" x 68" 15 Flower Blocks Three Rows of Five Each
Flower Colors Select colors based on Flower choices.	Two or Three fat eighths of each color Yellow, pink, blue, purple, orange, red	Two or Three fat quarters of each color Yellow, pink, blue, purple, orange, red
Optional – If you plan to make a Rainbow Border and/or Rainbow Bias Binding, cut these pieces first.	Rainbow Border (20) 2" x 8" pieces Bias Binding (18) 2¼" x 13" bias strips	Rainbow Border (26) 2" x 8" pieces Bias Binding (14) 2¼" x 22" bias strips
Stems and Leaves 　Dark Green and Medium Green	½ yd of each Cut from each 　(1) 16" x 20" piece for Stems 　(1) 3½" x 20" for Leaves	½ yd of each Cut from each 　(1) 16" x 20" piece for Stems 　(2) 3½" x 20" for Leaves
Accent Green	⅛ yd	⅛ yd
Optional Vine and Leaves for Border	¾ yd	1 yd
Quick Turn Appliqué 　Non-woven Fusible Interfacing 　Based on 22" width	1 yd 　(2) 3½" x 20" strips for Leaves 　Remainder for Flowers	1 yd 　(4) 3½" x 20" strips for Leaves 　Remainder for Flowers
100% Cotton Batting	⅛ yd	⅛ yd
Or Raw Edge Appliqué 　Paper backed fusible web Flowers 　Based on 17" width	1¾ yds 　(2) 16" x 20" pieces for Stems 　(2) 3½" x 20" strips for Leaves 　Remainder for Flowers	2½ yds 　(2) 16" x 20" pieces for Stems 　(4) 3½" x 20" strips for Leaves 　Remainder for Flowers
Optional Tear-Away Stabilizer Cut according to your product.	(6) 7½" squares	(15) 7½" squares
Background 　Blocks	½ yd 　(2) 7½" strips cut into 　　(6) 7½" squares	¾ yd 　(3) 7½" strips cut into 　　(15) 7½" squares
Lattice 　　Cut selvage to selvage 　Or Stripe 　　Cut lengthwise	⅔ yd 　(5) 3½" strips 1⅓ yds 　(1) 3½" strip for Inside Lattice 　(4) 5½" strips for Outside Lattice	1 yd 　(8) 3½" strips 1⅞ yds 　(2) 3½" strips for Inside Lattice 　(4) 5½" strips for Outside Lattice
Side and Corner Triangles	½ yd 　Cut later	1⅛ yds 　Cut later
Border	1 yd 　(5) 6½" strips	1½ yds 　(6) 8" strips
Scallop or Wave Binding 　One Fabric	½ yd 　(1) 16" strip cut into 　　(10) 2¼" bias strips	1 yd 　(2) 16" strips cut into 　　(14) 2¼" bias strips
Or Straight Binding 　One Fabric	½ yd 　(5) 3" strips	⅔ yd 　(7) 3" strips
Backing	1⅓ yds	3½ yds Cut into two equal parts
Batting	46" x 55"	62" x 75"

Yardage Chart for Blocks Set On Point with Lattice

Twin 70" x 98"	Full/Queen 92" x 100"	King 107" x 100"
21 Flower Blocks	35 Flower Blocks	42 Flower Blocks
Three Rows of Seven Each	Five Rows of Seven Each	Six Rows of Seven Each
Two or Three fat quarters of each color	**Two or Three fat quarters of each color**	**Two or Three fat quarters of each color**
Yellow, pink, blue, purple, orange, red	Yellow, pink, blue, purple, orange, red	Yellow, pink, blue, purple, orange, red
Rainbow Border (34) 2" x 8" pieces	Rainbow Border (40) 2" x 8" pieces	Rainbow Border (44) 2" x 8" pieces
Bias Binding (20) 2¼" x 22" bias strips	Bias Binding (23) 2¼" x 22" bias strips	Bias Binding (25) 2¼" x 22" bias strips
½ yd of each Cut from each	½ yd Cut from each	⅔ yd Cut from each
(1) 16" x 20" piece for Stems	(1) 16" x 20" piece for Stems	(1) 16" x 20" piece for Stems
(3) 3½" x 20" for Leaves	(4) 3½" x 20" for Leaves	(5) 3½" x 20" for Leaves
⅛ yd	⅛ yd	⅛ yd
1⅓ yds	1½ yds	1½ yds
2 yds	2¼ yds	3¼ yds
(6) 3½" x 20" strips for Leaves	(8) 3½" x 20" strips for Leaves	(10) 3½" x 20" strips for Leaves
Remainder for Flowers	Remainder for Flowers	Remainder for Flowers
¼ yd	¼ yd	¼ yd
3 yds	3¾ yds	4½ yds
(2) 16" x 20" pieces for Stems	(2) 16" x 20" pieces for Stems	(2) 16" x 20" pieces for Stems
(6) 3½" x 20" strips for Leaves	(8) 3½" x 20" strips for Leaves	(10) 3½" x 20" strips for Leaves
Remainder for Flowers	Remainder for Flowers	Remainder for Flowers
(21) 7½" squares	(35) 7½" squares	(42) 7½" squares
1¼ yds	1⅝ yds	2 yds
(5) 7½" strips cut into	(7) 7½" strips cut into	(9) 7½" strips cut into
(21) 7½" squares	(35) 7½" squares	(42) 7½" squares
1¼ yds	1¾ yds	2 yds
(10) 3½" strips	(16) 3½" strips	(18) 3½" strips
2⅝ yds	2⅝ yds	2⅝ yds
(2) 3½" strips for Inside Lattice	(4) 3½" strips for Inside Lattice	(2) 3½" strips for Inside Lattice
(4) 5½" strips for Outside Lattice	(4) 5½" strips for Outside Lattice	(4) 5½" strips for Outside Lattice
1⅛ yds	2 yds	2¼ yds
Cut later	Cut later	Cut later
3½ yds	4 yds	4¼ yds
(8) 14" strips	(9) 15" strips	(10) 15" strips
1 yd	1½ yd	1½ yds
(2) 16" strips cut into	(3) 16" strips cut into	(3) 16" strips cut into
(20) 2¼" bias strips	(23) 2¼" bias strips	(25) 2¼" bias strips
1 yd	1 yd	1 yd
(9) 3" strips	(11) 3" strips	(11) 3" strips
6 yds Cut into two equal parts	**8 yds** Cut into three equal parts	**9 yds** Cut into three equal parts
78" x 106"	98" x 108"	120" x 120"

General Instructions for all Quilts
Supplies

Open Toe Foot

InvisiGrip™ Cut a piece of InvisiGRIP™ ½" smaller than ruler. Place on bottom side of ruler. InvisiGRIP keeps the ruler from sliding when cutting.

¼" Foot

Steam Iron

Fine Point Permanent Marking Pen

Rotary Cutter and Cutting Mat

Check the permanence of your pen by drawing on smooth side of scrap interfacing and steam pressing dotted side of interfacing to scrap fabric. Substitute pen if it "runs" when pressed.

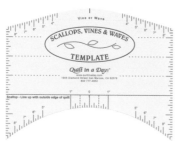

Scallops, Vines & Waves Template and Glow-Line™ Tape

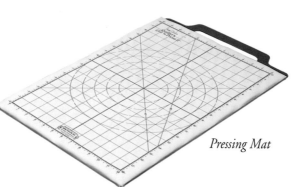
Pressing Mat

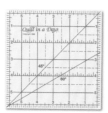

6" Square Up Ruler

Template Plastic

9½" Square Up Ruler

12½" Square Up Ruler

6" x 24" Ruler

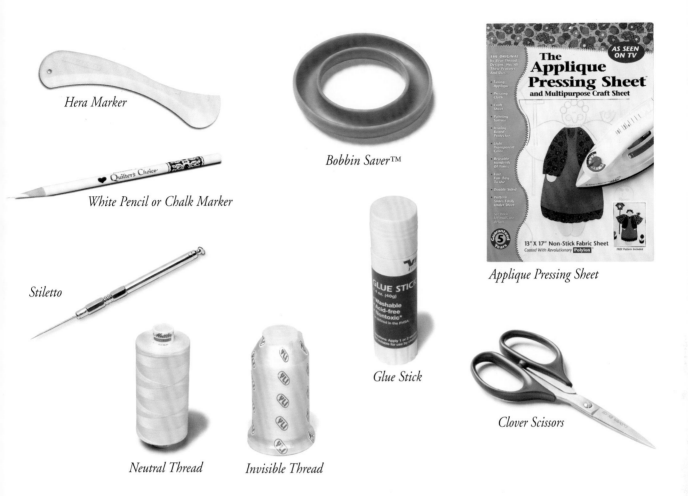

Hera Marker

White Pencil or Chalk Marker

Bobbin Saver™

Applique Pressing Sheet

Stiletto

Glue Stick

Clover Scissors

Neutral Thread

Invisible Thread

Applique Supplies for Quick Turn Flowers Only

Gather these supplies and tools for quick turning your Flowers with non-woven fusible interfacing. With this technique, the edges of the Flowers are turned under and can be hand or machine stitched in place.

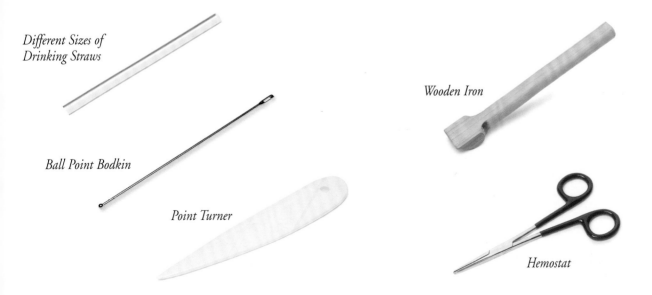

Different Sizes of Drinking Straws

Wooden Iron

Ball Point Bodkin

Point Turner

Hemostat

Cutting 7½" Background Squares

Regardless of which setting you choose, all Background squares are 7½". Refer to your Yardage Chart.

1. Place folded Background fabric on cutting mat. Straighten left edge.

2. Cut fabric into 7½" width strips selvage to selvage with 6" x 24" Ruler. Use lines on mat for measurement.

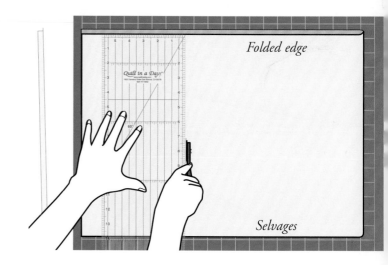

3. Turn strip and straighten left edge, trimming away selvages.

4. Layer cut strip into 7½" squares with 9½" Square Up Ruler.

5. To get a fifth 7½" square, open strip and cut on fold. *If you get crooked strips, try cutting with a Shape Cut™. You get fewer crooks in the middle of strips.*

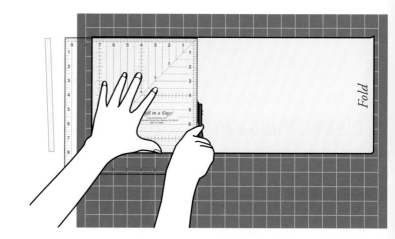

6. Stack squares right side up with stretch of grain across block. Blocks are easier to sew together if they all have the same stretch.

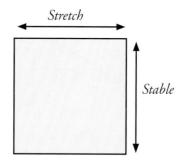

Making Leaf Templates

Each block has a Flower, a pair of Leaves, and a Stem that curves to the left or right.

Blocks in straight vertical rows have an Overlapping Leaf to connect Vines together.

Blocks Set in Straight Vertical Rows

Blocks on point do not need an Overlapping Leaf because there is no continuous Vine connecting them. However, they can be added to smaller Flowers if desired.

Blocks Set on Point

1. Make photocopy of pattern or patterns.

2. Cut a piece of template plastic the same size.

3. Using a glue stick, put glue on one side of template plastic. Place glue side of template plastic against print side of paper, and rub in place.

4. Cut out. If outside edges are rough, smooth with emery board.

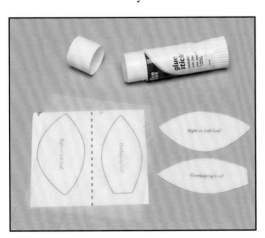

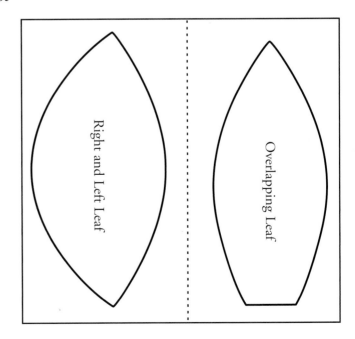

Right and Left Leaf

Overlapping Leaf

Marking Stem Placement for Straight Setting

Optional: You may want to photocopy all Placement Pages so you don't see images from the opposite side.

Stems curving to left   *Stems curving to right*

Light Background

1. Find desired Flower Placement Page. Flower patterns begin on page 68.

2. Place 7½" Background square on Placement Page, with stretch of grain across block.

3. Trace Stem line with pencil, extending line under Flower.

4. Mark each Flower independently as curves of Stems alternate between blocks.

5. Pin note on each block with name of Flower, or pencil name in seam allowance on wrong side.

Dark Background

1. Photocopy Placement Page.

2. Place 7½" Background square and Placement Page on light box.

3. Trace Stem lines with white pencil or white chalk.

4. If you do not have a light box, cut out Stem line on Placement Page, and use as a template to mark Stem.

Depending on placement of your Flower in row, you may need to change the direction of your Stems.

Marking Stem Placement for On Point Setting

1. Make photocopies of both On Point Placement Pages on pages 34 and 35.

2. Divide 7½" Background squares for your quilt into two stacks. One stack is for Stems curving to the left, and one stack is for Stems curving to the right.

*Stems
curving to the left*

*Stems
curving to the right*

3. Work on one stack at a time. Place 7½" Background square on Placement Page with Stem curving to the right.

4. Trace Stem line with pencil. Continue to mark stack.

5. Trace Stem lines curving to the left on the remaining stack of 7½" squares.

6. As you make your Flowers, check each Stem line. Some Stems may need to be lengthened as Wild Rose and Buttercup.

Stem Placement Pages for On Point Blocks

Stem curves to the right ⟶

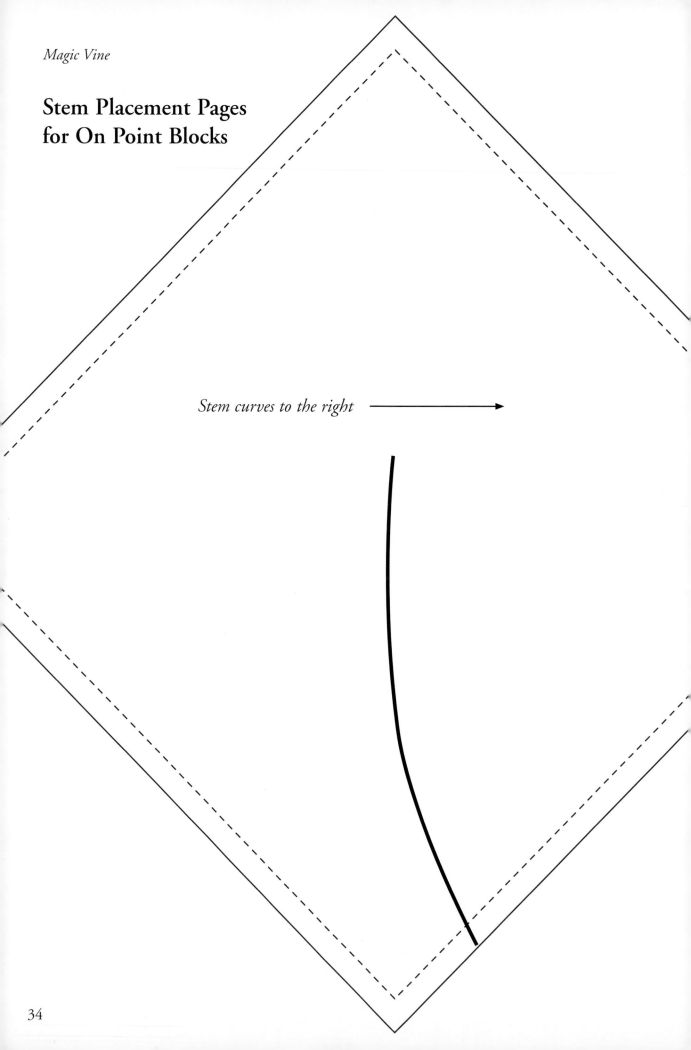

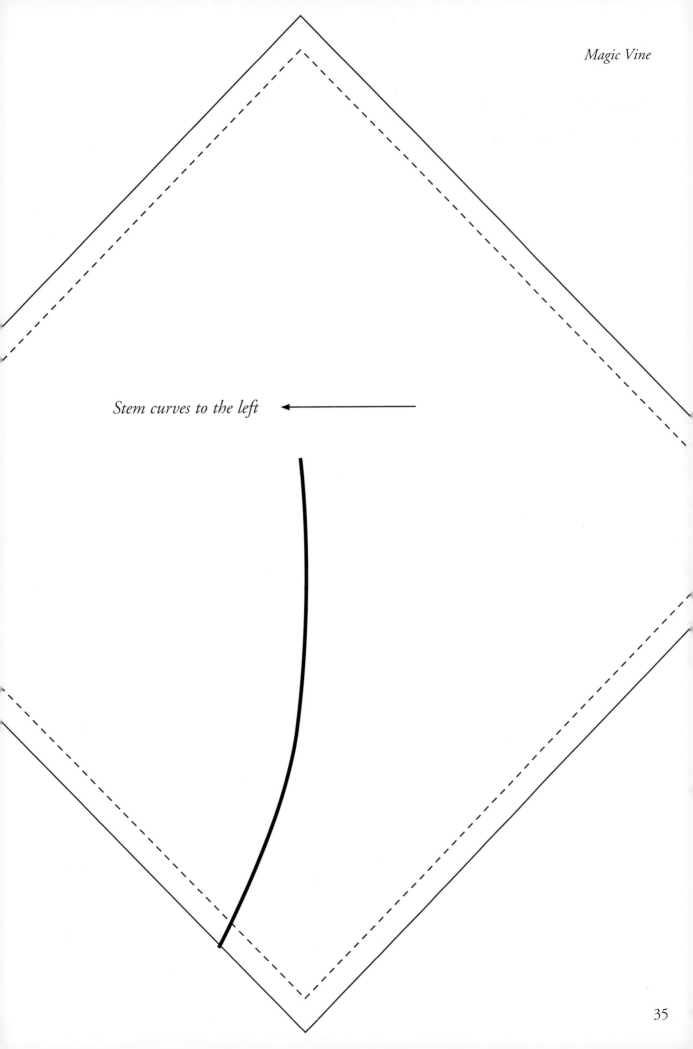

Stem curves to the left ←

Quick Turn Appliqué

This technique uses light to medium weight **non-woven fusible interfacing** and ultra fine point permanent markers such as .05 Pigma® Micron pens.

The interfacing has a smooth side and "dotted" side. Patterns are traced on the smooth side. The textured "dotted" side is the fusible side. The interfacing is sewn with the Flower fabric, and turned right side out so outside edges are finished.

Every Flower needs a pair of Leaves. Straight Set blocks need Overlapping Leaves. Most On Point blocks do not have Overlapping Leaves. If desired, make a few Overlapping Leaves for On Point blocks with smaller Flowers.

Patterns for Leaves are on page 31.

On Point blocks need a pair of Leaves. Leaves are connected to the Stem. If desired, make a few Overlapping Leaves for on point blocks with smaller Flowers.

Every Flower needs a pair of Leaves connected to the Stem. Straight Set blocks also need Overlapping Leaves to connect Stem together on the Vine.

Setting Up Your Sewing Machine

1. Load bobbins to match thread for Flowers, Leaves and Stems. Store in Bobbin Saver®.

2. Place thread matching the fabric on top and in the bobbin.

Store bobbins in Bobbin Saver®.

3. Reduce the pressure on the presser foot. Check your manual for instructions.

4. Select a straight stitch and center needle position on your sewing machine.

5. Set your machine with a small stitch, 15 stitches per inch or 1.8 on computerized sewing machine.

6. Use single hole throat plate for straight stitching. Use wide plate for decorative stitches.

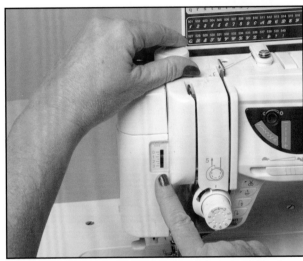

If possible, reduce the pressure on your presser foot.

7. Use an "open toe" metal or plastic foot with metal bottom to facilitate movement across the interfacing. A clear plastic foot tends to pucker the fusible interfacing at this step.

Making Bias Stems

Cutting Bias Stems

1. Cut one 16" x 20" strip from medium green and one from dark green. Refer to your Yardage Chart.

2. Line up 45º line on 6" x 24" Ruler across bottom edge.

3. Cut on diagonal. Fabric to left of diagonal cut can also be used for Stems.

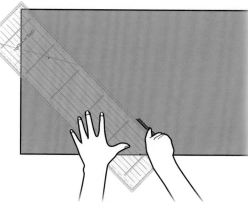

Line up 45º line on 6" x 24" Ruler across bottom edge.

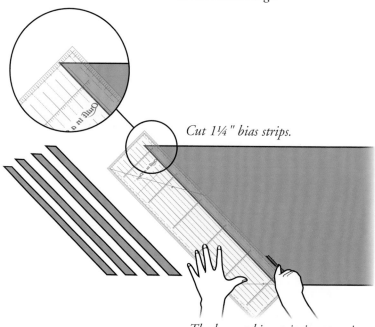

Cut 1¼" bias strips.

4. Turn ruler over. Move ruler over 1¼" from diagonal cut. Cut again.

5. Cut half of the 1¼" bias strips from medium green and half from dark green as needed.

The longest bias strip is approximately 23" long, and is enough for four to five Stems.

6. Press bias strips in half wrong sides together.

7. Store medium and dark Stems in separate marked plastic bags, and use appropriate green when making Stems.

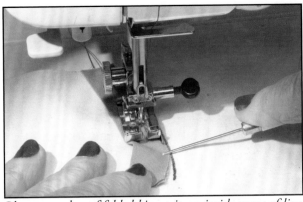

Sewing Stems from Bias Strips

1. Cut 1¼" bias strips to length indicated on each individual Flower Placement Page. Trace Stem if you haven't already.

2. Place raw edges of folded bias strip on **inside curve of line.**

3. **Allow ½" to hang over on edge to compensate for the angle after its turned back.**

Place raw edges of folded bias strip on inside curve of line.

4. **Sew scant ¼" seam.** Use a stiletto to hold Stem in place.

5. If Stem curves to the right, sew Stem from bottom up.

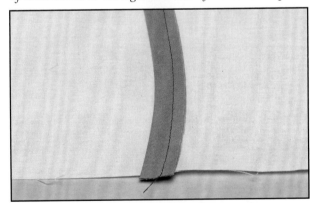

If Stem curves to the right, sew Stem from bottom up.

6. If Stem curves to the left, sew Stem from top down.

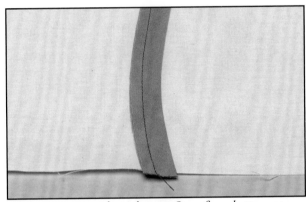

If Stem curves to the left, sew Stem from top down.

7. Fold bias strip back over raw edge and press flat. Stem should cover raw edge without trimming. If necessary, decrease the width of your seam allowance.

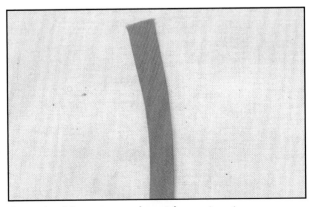

Stem should cover raw edge without trimming.

Machine Blind Hem Stitch

1. Place thread matching Stem on top and in bobbin.

2. For invisible thread, loosen top tension and use bobbin thread to match Background.

3. Take straight stitches on Background, and narrow "bite" into Stem.

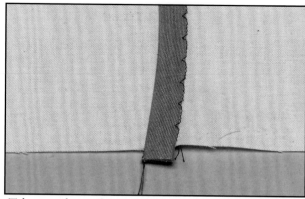

Take straight stitches on Background, and narrow bite into Stem.

Hand Appliqué

1. Thread a fine hand sewing needle with a single strand of thread matching green. Knot end of thread.

2. Push threaded needle through fold from wrong side.

3. Pull needle completely through fold.

4. Push needle through Background next to place where needle came out.

5. Move forward on underneath side of Background and repeat stitch.

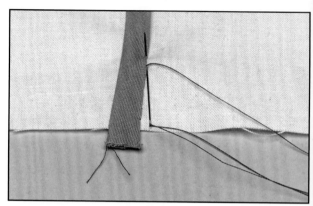

A 60 count 100% silk thread disappears into the fabric. Waxed thread does not tangle.

Rickrack Stem

Use ½" or ¾" wide rickrack as an alternative for a fabric Stem. Purchase 6" rickrack for each Flower.

1. Center rickrack on Stem line.

2. Sew down center of rickrack with wide zigzag stitch and open toe applique foot.

3. You can also topstitch both sides of rickrack 1/16" from edges.

Yardage for Rickrack

	Flower Stems
Wallhanging	1¾ yds
Lap	2¼ yds
Twin	5 yds
Full/Queen	7¼ yds
King	8½ yds

Tracing Leaves for
One Straight Set Block or One On Point Block

Patterns for Leaves are on page 31.

1. Cut 3½" x 4½" piece fusible interfacing and
   3½" x 4½" piece green fabric.

2. One template is used for the pair of Leaves.
   Trace two Leaves on smooth side of interfacing with permanent marking pen. Leave ⅜"
   between Leaves.

3. Place fusible side of interfacing against right side
   of fabric, and pin.

4. Sewing instructions begin on page 44.

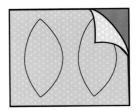

3½" x 4½"

Tracing Overlapping Leaf for
One Straight Set Block

1. Trace one Overlapping Leaf on smooth side
   of 2" x 3½" interfacing.

2. Pair fusible side of interfacing against right side
   of 2" x 3½" fabric, and pin.

2" x 3½"

Assembly-Line Tracing Pairs of Leaves
for Straight Set and On Point Blocks

*One Leaf template is used for the pair of Leaves connected to the Stem. It's best to
have all Leaves ready before starting the Flowers.*

1. Place 3½" strip non-woven fusible interfacing **smooth side up.** Place on top
   of cardboard so permanent marking pen does not mark surface underneath.

2. Trace two Leaves for each
   Flower on smooth side of
   interfacing with permanent
   marking pen. **Leave ⅜"
   between Leaves.**

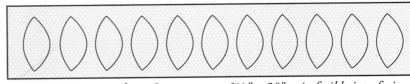

You can trace ten to eleven Leaves on one 3½" x 20" strip fusible interfacing.

3. Place 3½" strips of medium green and dark green fabric right side up.

4. Place fusible side of 3½" strips interfacing against right side of each fabric, and pin.

5. Sewing instructions begin on page 44.

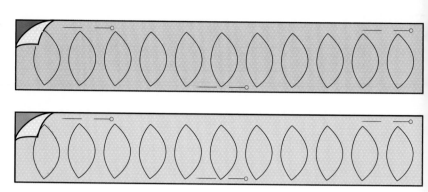

Overlapping Leaves for Straight Set Blocks Only

The on Point blocks do not need overlapping leaves. However, you may choose to add a few here and there.

1. Place 3½" strip fusible interfacing smooth side up. Place Leaf template with **flat side against bottom edge**. Trace Leaves on interfacing with permanent marking pen, leaving ⅜" between Leaves. Mark one Leaf for each Flower.

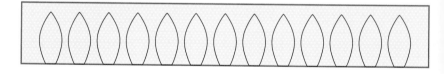

2. Place 3½" strips of medium green and dark green fabric right side up. Place fusible side of 3½" strips interfacing against right side of each fabric, and pin.

3. Sewing instructions begin on page 44.

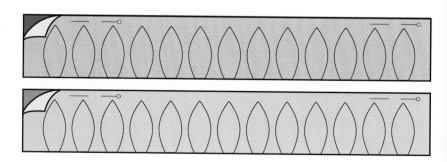

Making Flowers

Instructions for individual Flowers begin on page 68.

1. Cut one piece of interfacing the same size as the group of pattern pieces. Place fusible interfacing on the pattern sheet with **smooth side up.** Place on top of white paper so the surface underneath is not marked.

2. Trace pieces with a fine point permanent marking pen. Include dashed lines.

Trace patterns on smooth side of fusible interfacing with permanent marking pen.

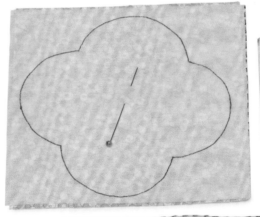

3. Cut interfacing pieces apart on **long dashed lines.** Do not cut around Flowers.

4. Cut fabric for Flowers in designated colors and sizes.

5. Place fabric **right side up.**

6. Place each interfacing piece on corresponding fabric piece with **dotted fusible side against right side of fabric.** The smooth side of interfacing is on top.

If desired, center a Flower in the circle for a "fussy cut."

7. Pin in the center of each pattern piece. **Do not press.**

Sewing Around Each Pattern Piece

1. Begin sewing in the middle of a side. Sew on the inside edge of the line so you don't see the line after the Flower is turned.

2. Slowly sew on curved lines lifting the presser foot and turning the pieces as necessary. Pivot with the needle in the fabric.

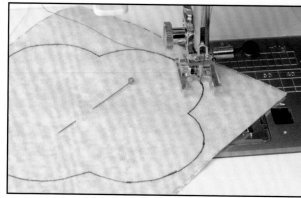

Use the "needle down" feature. The needle stops in the fabric each time you stop sewing. This feature makes it easy to control sewing on curves and when pivoting.

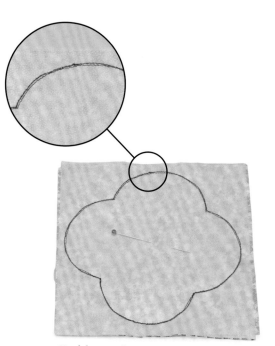

3. End by overlapping stitches.

End by overlapping stitches.

4. Some pieces have an open side. Backstitch on ends and leave open where indicated.

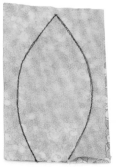

Leave open where indicated with dashed lines.

Trimming Each Piece

1. Using sharp, pointed trimming scissors, trim each piece ⅛" from the stitching.

2. Trim corners, and clip inside curves and outside points.

Turning Pieces Without Open Side

1. Pull fusible interfacing away from fabric.

2. Carefully cut a small slit the size of a straw through fusible interfacing only.

3. Cut slits across the width on the Leaves.

4. Cut drinking straw in half, and insert straw into slit. Place straw against fabric.

Use very narrow straw for smallest pieces, and ¼" wide straw for most pieces.

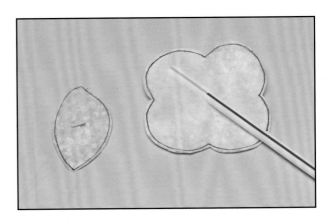

5. Stretch fabric over end of straw. Place ball of bodkin on stretched fabric and gently push fabric into straw about 1" with bodkin. This technique begins to turn the piece.

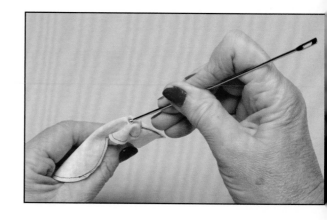

6. Remove straw and bodkin.

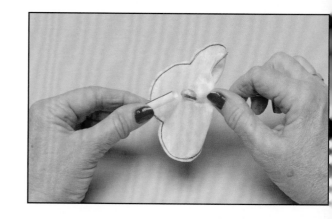

7. If necessary, repeat turning second half with straw and bodkin. Finish turning with fingers.

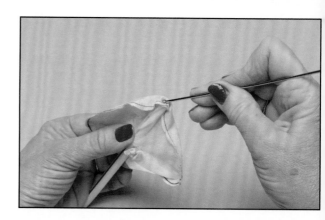

8. Push out edges by running bodkin around inside.

   You could also use curved side of point turner on larger pieces.

Turning Pieces with Open Side

1. Insert straw into opening. Place straw against fabric.

2. Push fabric into straw with bodkin and turn right side out.

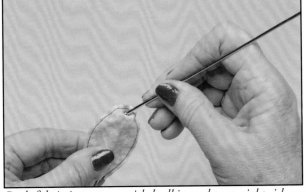

Push fabric into straw with bodkin and turn right side out.

3. Pull out points with stiletto or pin.

4. If you accidentally poke a hole in the edge of the Flower, see page 95 for repair technique.

Pull out points with stiletto or pin.

Pressing Pieces

Before Flowers are permanently pressed onto 7½" Background squares, press fabric edges so interfacing does not show. Select either method.

Wooden Iron

1. Press fabric edges with a small wooden "pressing stick," called a wooden iron.

2. Beginning from center on right side, push fabric over interfacing edge.

Push fabric over interfacing edge.

Appliqué Pressing Sheet

1. Place Flower right side up on pressing sheet.

2. Steam press.

3. Peel Flower off appliqué pressing sheet.

It's important to press the fabric over the edges so interfacing is not visible from right side.

Stuffing With Cotton Batting

1. Using the turned piece as a pattern, cut 100% cotton batting into the same shape and size. *Sewing batting with the appliqué results in bulky edges.*

2. Insert batting through opening with hemostat. Smooth edges.

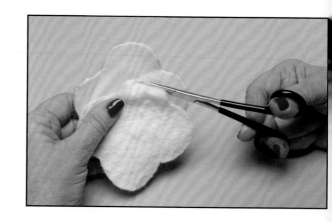

Pressing Pieces in Place

Straight Set Blocks

1. Put Placement Page on pressing mat. Position 7½" Background square on Placement Page.

2. Position pieces on Background, following outline of Placement Page underneath. Tuck raw edges under finished pieces. **Place Leaves touching Stems.**

On blocks set in straight vertical rows, the top block on each row does not have an Overlapping Leaf.

On Point Blocks

1. Position 7½" Background square on point on pressing mat.

2. Position pieces on Background, carefully overlapping appropriate pieces. Place **Leaves touching Stems.** Make sure edges of Leaves are at least ½" from edges of Background.

Only as a visual guide, refer to Placement Page of that Flower.

Pressing Pieces

1. If used, carefully slide out Placement Page.

2. Using a cotton setting and steam, firmly press Flower and pair of Leaves to the Background.

3. Use straight down and up motion with steam iron. Give block a shot of steam when iron is on Flower.

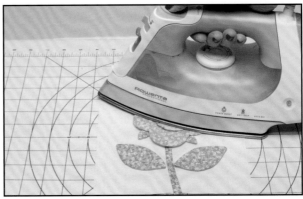

If desired, place appliqué pressing sheet over block to prevent possible scorching and dirt from iron.

4. For blocks with Overlapping Leaf, **press only bottom half of Leaf.** Slip Appliqué pressing sheet under top half to prevent fusing.

5. Once pieces fuse, turn over and press from wrong side. "Stuffed pieces" may refuse to bond. If so, pin after attempted pressing.

6. If you are not satisfied with any placement, repress, peel the piece off, reposition and press again.

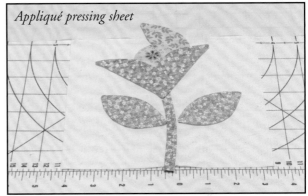

Appliqué pressing sheet

Do not press top half of Overlapping Leaf.

Blocks in Straight Vertical Rows

It's important to use the Placement Page for each block so Overlapping Leaves on Vines line up when blocks are sewn together.

If you create your own arrangement of Flowers, plan your placement before pressing. Place the first block with Flower, Stem, and pair of Leaves. Then place a second block with another Flower and pair of Leaves. Put the two blocks together at the seam. Slip the Overlapping Leaf under the top of the second Flower, and manipulate it to cover the first Stem.

As an option, leave top of Flowers open. Insert Overlapping Leaf after sewing blocks together. Sew Leaf in place last.

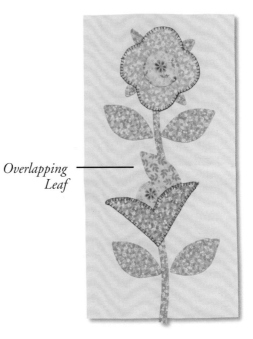

Overlapping Leaf

Sewing Outside Edges by Machine

1. Place #11 needle in your sewing machine.

2. Select a stitch as blind hem or blanket stitch, and sew outside edges of Flower on test block.

3. If block ripples from stitch you select, pin a 7½" square of tear-away stabilizer under Background square.

Pin a square of stabilizer under block.

Blind Hem Stitch

1. Place matching thread or invisible thread on your machine. If you use invisible thread, loosen top tension and use bobbin thread to match Background.

2. Select blind hem stitch. Take straight stitches on Background, and narrow "bite" into Flower. Adjust stitch width so bite just barely catches fabric.

3. **On Straight Set blocks, finish outside edges of all pieces but Overlapping Leaf.**

Edge marking can be coaxed under with a stiletto or pinned under and then stitched over.

Blanket Stitch

1. Place thread darker than Flower on top and in bobbin, or contrasting thread.

2. Select blanket stitch. Take straight stitches on Background, and narrow "bite" into Flower.

3. Pivot on curves with your needle down on outside edge.

4. **On Straight Set blocks, finish outside edges of all pieces but Overlapping Leaf.**

Try a blanket stitch with a 3.5 stitch width and 2.5 stitch length on your machine to see if stitch covers edges.

Sewing Outside Edges by Hand

With the Quick Turn method, outside edges of the
Flowers are soft, and can easily be hand appliquéd in place.

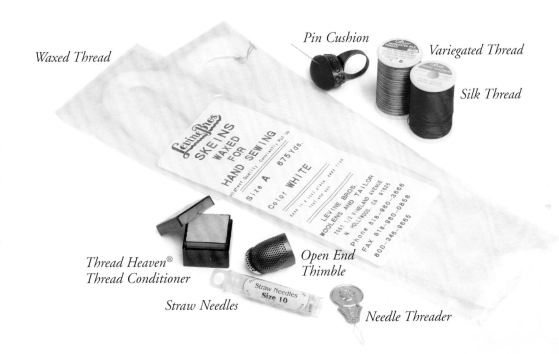

Waxed Thread

Pin Cushion

Variegated Thread

Silk Thread

Thread Heaven®
Thread Conditioner

Open End
Thimble

Straw Needles

Needle Threader

Hand Appliqué

There are many threads, thimbles, and needles available. You will need to experiment
and decide which you prefer.

You can choose to use long thin needles, as a size 10 or 11 straw needle or appliqué
needles in sizes 10 to 12 referred to as sharps.

Try 100% silk thread in 60 wt. for a stitch that disappears into the fabric. For thread
that doesn't tangle, try waxed thread. For similar results, run regular thread through
Thread Heaven®, a thread conditioner.

Thimbles are a personal choice. Pick your favorite from plastic, leather, silver, gold, open
end, and ones with ridges.

Threading Needles

1. Most hand sewing needles can be threaded with the use of a needle threader. A wooden base is available to hold the threader in place.

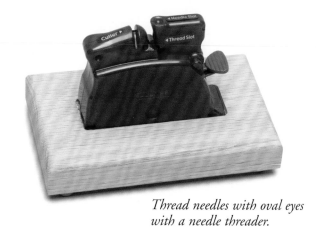

Thread needles with oval eyes with a needle threader.

2. Place needle with eye in needle slot. It must be an oval eye with needle the thickness from .51 - .89 mm. A circular eye needle can not be threaded.

3. Set thread in thread slot.

4. Holding onto the threader, press lever softly while holding thread gently.

   Two strands of embroidery floss can be threaded into an oval eye of an embroidery needle. If thick thread that is not applicable to needle thickness is used, it may not thread.

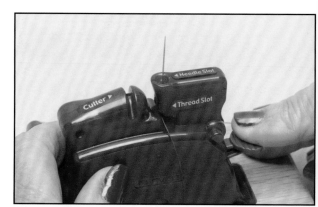

Place needle with eye in needle slot, set thread in thread slot, and gently press lever.

5. Carefully pull out threaded needle. Continue to pull thread through needle.

6. Cut thread to desired length with thread cutter.

Pull thread through needle.

Making the Blind Hem Stitch or Hidden Appliqué Stitch

1. Select thread matching Flower. If you are unable to find an exact color match of thread, use a shade lighter if appliquéing a Flower to a light background. Use a shade darker if you are appliquéing to a dark background.

2. Put thimble on your finger.

3. Knot the end of a single thread, and bring up your needle from underneath the Background fabric, barely catching the fabric edge of the Flower.

4. Insert the needle back into the Background fabric, directly opposite where you came out and just over the edge of the Flower being sewn on.

5. Bring the needle back up through the fabrics, about ¹/₁₆th of an inch away from the previous stitch. Continue taking tiny stitches all the way around the piece.

6. Bring thread to the back, and knot.

7. Finish outside edges of all pieces but Overlapping Leaf.

Hand Embroidery Stitches

Use embroidery floss or #5 to #8 pearl cotton plus a large eyed, embroidery needle and needle threader. The higher the number the finer the pearl cotton. For instance, #8 pearl cotton pulls through fabric easier, while #5 makes a heavier, showy looking stitch.

Needle Threader

Braiding Floss

1. Pull off paper rings on embroidery floss. Wrap single strand floss around hand to elbow, which is approximately 22". Lay floss flat on table and cut both ends.

2. Once all colors are prepared, have one person hold ends together while second person braids floss.

3. When needed, pull out a single strand of floss. The braid bunches as you remove strand, but can be pulled out flat.

Starting Floss without Braiding

1. To get a new package of embroidery floss started, find the end tucked **on the inside** of the skein. Pull off two loops, or approximately 22". Cut in the crease.

2. For most embroidery stitches, divide out two strands of embroidery floss.

Blanket Stitch

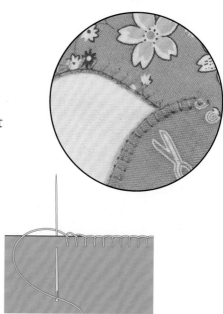

1. Thread embroidery needle with one strand of #8 pearl cotton, or two stands of embroidery floss, and knot.

2. Bring floss from back side of Background square to front on edge of Flower.

3. Hold floss along top edge of Flower, with end pointing the direction you are going to embroider.

4. Make a loop pointing upward. Insert needle in and out of fabric. As the needle exits from the wrong side, bring needle through the loop of floss. Tighten your stitch, keeping floss on edge of Flower with your fingernail.

French Knots

1. Use one strand of #8 pearl cotton or two to three strands of embroidery floss. Bring needle up through fabric at the point where the knot is to be made.

2. Hold the needle close to the fabric and wind the floss two or three times around the point. If you want a large knot, wind five times.

3. Hold the floss taut around the needle and insert the needle through the fabric close to the point where the floss came out. Place your thumb over the knot to hold the twist in place and pull the floss through to the underside, bringing the knot snugly against the fabric.

4. Make as many French Knots as desired.

5. Knot on the back side.

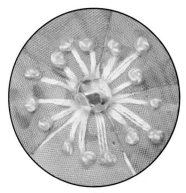

Center of Wild Rose

Satin Stitch Center

1. Draw small circle in center of Flower.

2. Bring needle threaded with floss up at one edge of circle, and insert at opposite edge. Sew through fabric only.

3. Return to starting line by carrying floss underneath fabric. Make stitches close enough together to cover circle completely.

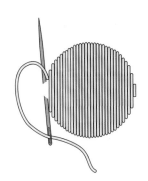

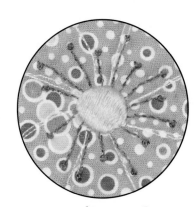

Center of Bouncing Bet

Stem Stitch

1. Working from left to right, take regular small stitches along the line.

2. Emerge the thread on the left side of the previous stitch. Use this stitch for Flower stems, pistils, outlines, and a filling worked closely together.

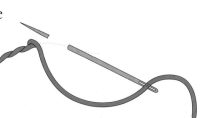

Center of Arrowhead

Lazy Daisy

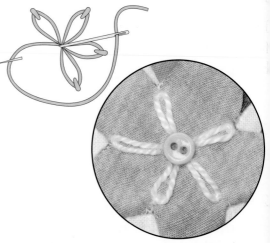

1. Thread an embroidery needle with floss or pearl cotton and knot on the backside. Visually divide Flower into five parts.

2. Bring thread up in the center. Re-insert needle in center, and exit needle at end of first daisy Petal.

3. Loop floss around needle and pull gently, keeping loop shape.

4. Push needle back down at end of loop, holding it in place.

5. Continue coming up from center, wrapping floss around needle and pulling gently.

6. Sew a button or French knots in center.

Center of Forget Me Not

Backstitch

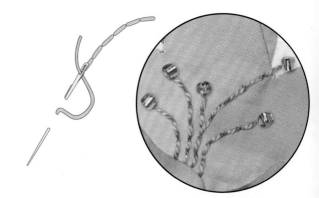

1. Thread embroidery needle with two stands of floss or pearl cotton, knot, and bring needle up to right side.

2. Take one stitch to right, and exit needle one stitch length behind that stitch.

3. Make connected line of stitches without overlapping.

Center of Tiger Lily

Fill In Stitch for Stars

1. Trace Star on template plastic, and cut out.

2. Place template on center of Flower, and trace.

3. Thread hand sewing needle with two strands of black embroidery floss, or one strand of #8 pearl cotton.

4. From the center of the Star to the point, take a long stitch to create a point, and then take smaller stitches on each side.

Center of Phlox

Bead Embellishment

Hand sew beads or buttons to Flowers after the top is quilted. Use beads to fill centers, or for pistils and stamens. Suggested beads to use are bugle beads, transparent glass beads, seed beads, sequins, pearls, and bicone Swarovski® crystal beads.

1. Select a needle slender enough to pass through the hole in the bead. Try a beading needle that is long, thin and flexible. If beading needle is too flimsy for the thickness, try a #12 or #10 quilting between needle.

2. Select a beading thread as Silamide or Nimo that doesn't tangle and comes in a variety of colors. Beading thread is a strong nylon thread which does not fray or separate while beading. Purchase thread to match the color of the beads, not the fabric.

3. Thread needle, and knot double strands on the end.

4. Pull needle up through fabric, slip on a bead, insert needle back into fabric, and pull it through to wrong side.

5. Knot thread on backside before sewing on the next bead. If thread should accidentally break on one bead, only that one bead will come loose, and not the others.

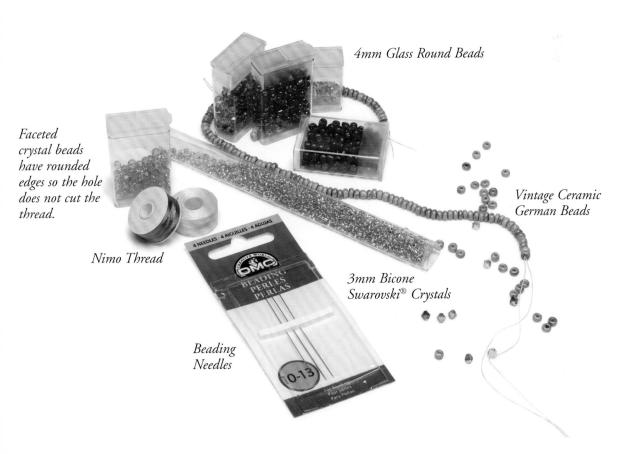

4mm Glass Round Beads

Faceted crystal beads have rounded edges so the hole does not cut the thread.

Vintage Ceramic German Beads

Nimo Thread

3mm Bicone Swarovski® Crystals

Beading Needles

Raw Edge Appliqué

This technique uses **paper backed fusible web** to fuse Flowers to Background squares. The outside edges of Flowers are raw so stitches are sewn over them.

Milkwort made with Quick Turn technique

Milkwort made with Raw Edge technique

When you do this method, Flowers appear reversed when fused in place. Most Flowers do not appear obviously different except for the Milkwort, Tiger Lily, Nasturtium, and Poppy.

Check to see if your photocopier has a Mirror Image selection. If you photocopy your patterns in mirror image, they will finish exactly as they appear on the Placement Page.

Making Bias Stems

You may want to make your Stems with finished edges rather than raw edges. In that case, follow directions on page 38 for bias stems cut 1¼" wide. Directions are also included for marking stems on dark fabric.

Cutting Bias Stems

1. Cut one 16" x 20" medium green and one from dark green. Cut pieces of paper backed fusible web the same size. Refer to your Yardage Chart.

2. Place fabric wrong side up on pressing mat. Place fusible side of paper backed web against wrong side of fabric.

3. Fuse in place following manufacturer's directions.

4. Line up 45º line on 6" x 24" Ruler with bottom edge.

5. Cut on diagonal. Fabric to left of cut can be used for Stems.

6. Turn ruler over. Move ruler over ⅜" from diagonal cut. Cut again.

7. Cut ⅜" bias strips as needed.

8. Store medium and dark Stems in separate plastic bags, and use when directions call for Stem strips.

Line up outside edges of fusible web with wrong side of fabric, and fuse in place.

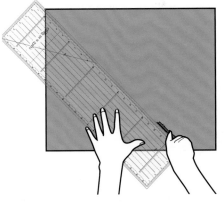

Line up 45º line on 6" x 24" Ruler with bottom edge.

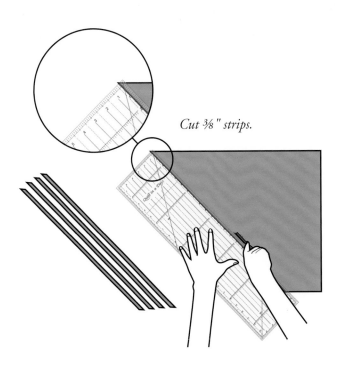

Cut ⅜" strips.

Fusing Stems for Straight Setting

Optional: You may want to photocopy all Placement Pages beginning on page 69.

1. Mark Stems on 7½" Background squares following directions on page 32.

2. Trace Stem line with pencil, extending line under Flower. Mark each Flower independently as curves of Stems alternate between blocks.

3. Cut ⅜" bias strip to length indicated on each individual Placement Page. Peel off paper.

4. **Center on line**, and fuse in place. **Allow ½" to hang over edge.**

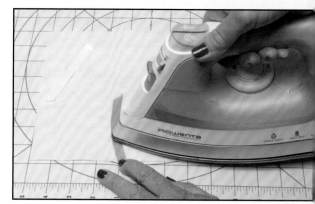

Fusing Stems for On Point Setting

1. Mark Stems on 7½" Background squares following directions on pages 33 to 35.

2. Divide 7½" Background squares into two stacks for Stems curving to the left, and Stems curving to the right.

3. Cut ⅜" bias strip to length needed, and peel off paper.

4. Center on line, and fuse in place. **Allow ½" to hang over edge.**

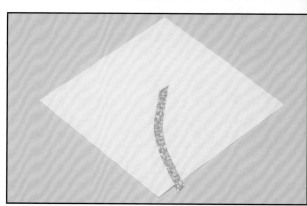

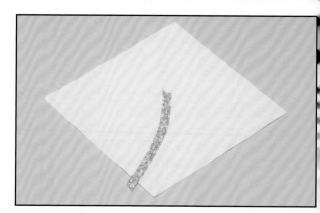

Finishing Edges of Bias Stems

Straight Stitch

1. Use green thread matching your Stems on top and in bobbin.

2. Sew straight stitch lines ⅛" in from both edges.

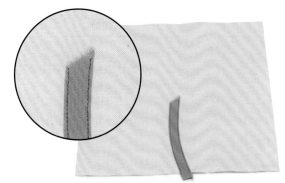

Blanket Stitch

1. Use green thread matching your Stems on top and in bobbin.

2. Use needle down position. Sew straight stitch on Background, and "bite" into Stem.

3. Pivot on curves with needle down on outside edges.

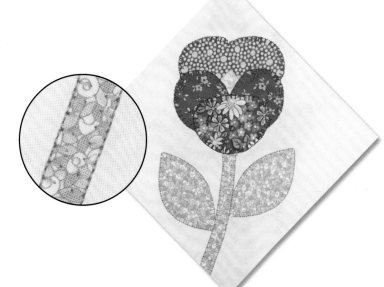

Satin Stitch

1. Use green thread matching your Stems on top and in bobbin.

2. Optional: Prepare Leaves following directions on page 62. Fuse Stems and Leaves at same time.

3. Begin with a locking stitch. For satin stitch, use a very closely spaced zigzag stitch. Sew satin stitch continuously around Stem and Leaves without cutting thread.

4. For efficiency, stitch Stems and Leaves for all Flowers at same time.

Making Leaves

Leaf patterns are on page 31.
One Leaf template can be used on either the left or right side of the Stem.

Right and Left Leaves for all Flowers

1. Place 3½" strip paper backed fusible web paper side up. Trace Leaves on paper side with permanent marking pen. Leave ¼" between Leaves. Trace two Leaves for each Flower. You can trace eleven Leaves on one 3½" x 20" strip.

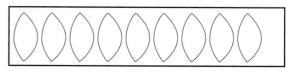

2. Place 3½" strips of medium green and dark green fabric **wrong side up**. Place bumpy fusible side of web on **wrong side of fabric**.

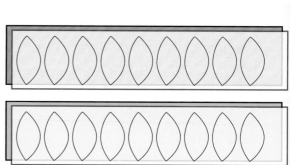

3. Fuse in place following manufacturer's directions. Be careful not to get fusing on iron.

Overlapping Leaves for Straight Set Blocks Only

1. Place 3½" strip fusible web with paper side up. Trace Overlapping Leaf with flat side against bottom edge. Mark one Leaf for each Flower, minus the Leaf on the top of each row.

2. Place 3½" green fabric strips wrong side up. Place bumpy fusible side of web on **wrong side of fabric**.

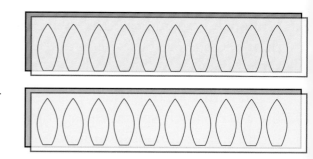

3. Fuse in place following manufacturer's directions. Be careful not to get fusing on iron.

4. Cut out Leaves with sharp pair of scissors.

5. Store two colors of Leaves in separate plastic bags.

Making Flowers

1. Cut a piece of paper backed fusible web the same size as the group of pattern pieces. The piece is generally 5" x 7½".

2. Place fusible web with **paper side up** on pattern pieces, and trace around each pattern with a pencil or permanent marking pen.

Trace patterns on paper side of fusible web.

3. To use less fusible web, reposition paper each time to trace another shape. Allow at least ½" between shapes.

   If you want to do hand stitches in the center of the Flower, cut out circle of paper and web before fusing.

Trace patterns on paper side of fusible web.

4. Rough cut around shapes with at least ¼" fusible beyond marked lines.

5. Following each Yardage Chart, select Flower colors and cut designated sizes of pieces.

6. Place fabric **wrong side up** on pressing mat. Center rough side of fusible pattern on wrong side of fabric.

7. Fuse in place following the manufacturer's guidelines. Allow pieces to cool.

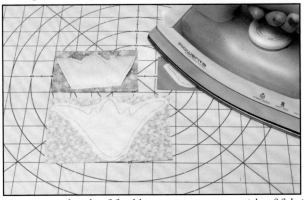
Center rough side of fusible pattern on wrong side of fabric.

8. Using sharp scissors, cut out each shape on the pencil line.

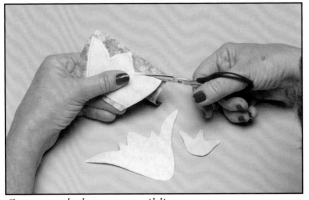
Cut out each shape on pencil line.

9. Peel off paper backing by running your fingernail across the edge of the paper, or scratch the paper with a pin.

Peel off paper.

Pressing Straight Set Blocks

1. Put Placement Page on pressing mat. Position 7½" Background square on Placement Page.

2. Position pieces on Background, following outline of Placement Page underneath. Carefully overlap appropriate pieces. Place Leaves touching stem.

3. If block has an Overlapping Leaf, put Appliqué pressing sheet under top half of Leaf.

4. Following manufacturer's instructions, fuse pieces in place.

Fuse pieces in place.

Pressing on Point Blocks

1. Position 7½" Background square on point on pressing mat.

2. Position Flower pieces on Background, carefully overlapping appropriate pieces. Place Leaves touching Stems. Make sure edges of Leaves are at least ½" away from outside edges of Background square.

3. Following manufacturer's instructions, fuse pieces in place.

Only as a visual guide, refer to Placement Page for that Flower.

Hint: If you accidentally get fusible web on the bottom of your iron, clean it with a commercial cleaner. In a pinch, you can also use a dryer sheet such as Bounce®. After the bottom of your iron is clean, crumple up the dryer sheet and rub it across your appliqué sheet to remove excess fusing.

Sewing Outside Edges by Machine

Setting Up Your Machine

1. Put a #10 microtex needle in your machine. Other needles to test are Schmetz® embroidery needles, and stitch nadel embroidery needles 75/11.

2. Thread your machine with slightly darker or contrasting thread on top and in the bobbin. Variegated thread also gives a nice finish.

3. Pin four corners of tear-away stabilizer underneath practice block.

4. Select one of these machine stitches to cover raw edges.

   - Blanket Stitch
   - Satin Stitch
   - Combination of Two
   - Straight Stitch

5. Once block is finished, use seam ripper to help tear away stabilizer.

Practice with and without stabilizer to see if outside edges of Flower pucker. Check to see that stabilizer can easily be torn away.

Blanket Stitch

1. Use needle down position. Select blanket stitch. Take straight stitches on Background, and narrow "bite" into Flower.

3. Pivot on curves with your needle down on outside edge.

4. **Finish outside edges of all pieces but Overlapping Leaf.**

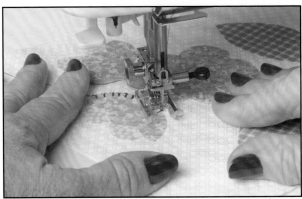

This blanket stitch is set at 3.5 width and 2.5 length.

Satin Stitch

1. Select a zigzag stitch. Work with stitch width and length to get a very closely spaced zigzag stitch. Try a 2.2 width and .4 length to see if you get good coverage.

2. Write down whatever setting you decide so you can always return to that setting. Practice, paying close attention to the way stitches are made. Change needle half way through project to avoid dull needle.

3. Find a straight or slightly curved edge of Flower. Place needle down on outside edge of appliqué.

4. Begin sewing by looking in front of presser foot instead of at needle. Start with pieces on the bottom of layers, and work toward the top. That way, each new line of stitching will cover the ends of the preceding stitches, leaving a clean finish.

5. To rip out poor satin stitches, put a sharp seam ripper under stitches on wrong side of block. Push tip of ripper under stitches, lift up, and cut stitches.

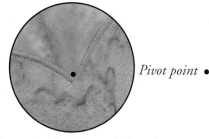

Pivot point •

On an inside corner, stitch to the point and stop with needle down. Pivot and continue stitching. Notice how there are no satin stitches inside the V.

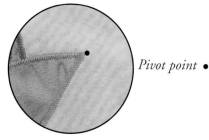

Pivot point •

On an outside corner, stitch to end of appliqué, and stop with needle down on outside edge of appliqué. Lift presser foot and pivot. Lower presser foot and continue stitching on new edge.

Machine Stitch on Leaves

1. Select lightning or triple stitch.

2. Curve stitch down center of first Leaf, raise presser foot to skip Stem, and curve stitch second Leaf.

3. For efficiency, stitch all Leaves at same time.

Combination of Two Stitches

1. Select stitch that is a combination of the satin stitch and blanket stitch.

2. Experiment with stitch settings for your machine. Try 3.5 stitch length and .35 stitch width to see if stitches cover raw edges.

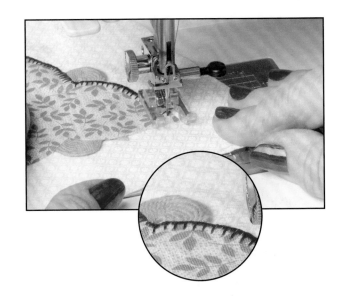

Straight Stitch

1. Select straight stitch. Use needle down feature.

2. Sew ⅛" away from outside edge.

3. To make pivoting easier, place a darning foot on sewing machine, and drop feed dogs.

4. Free motion stitch around Flowers. For decoration, stitch around Flower several times. Free motion stitching can be done before or after layering quilt with batting and backing.

Embellishing Centers of Flowers

To hand embellish Flower centers with embroidery stitches, buttons, or beads, refer to pages 54 to 57.

Evening Primrose

First Pattern in Attractive Vine Quilt

Suppose we start on the first block. The Evening Primrose is light yellow in color. The sepals, those four dark projecting points, are of the same shade of green as the leaves and stems.

The center may be a deeper yellow than the petals or it may be of plain yellow to contrast with the figured material used in the Flower. Or plain, soft yellow may be used for Flower and figured for the center.

In choosing the greens used in this quilt get two shades. One shade will be used in this first vine for leaves and stem and the lighter shade will be the color chosen for the overlapping leaf which will join one block to another. You get a hint of that leaf in the dotted portion at the base of the stem. Nancy told the club members that she would explain this leaf at the next meeting.

A block just like this is used in the third vine of the quilt so the members made a duplicate of the first block while they had cloth and patterns at hand.

Copyright, 1930

1. Optional: Photocopy page and place on light table.

2. Place 7½" Background square on Placement Page.

3. Trace Stem line.

4. Cut 4" long bias Stem and sew to Background square with your chosen method.

Yardage and Patterns

Cut one set for each block.

 Petals
Light Yellow
4" x 4½"

 Center
Deeper Yellow
2½" square

 Sepals
Green
1¼" x 4½"
or 12" of ⅜" Ribbon

 Leaves and Stem
Green
3½" x 4"
4" bias

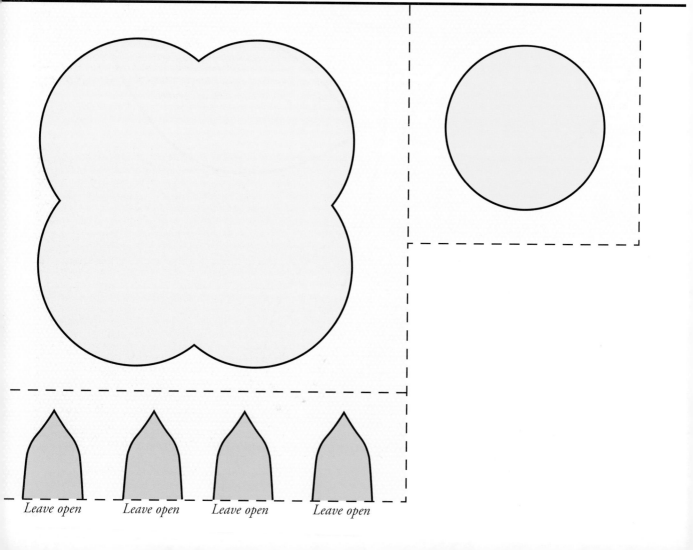

Leave open   *Leave open*   *Leave open*   *Leave open*

Quick Turn Flowers: Follow general directions on pages 36-57.
Raw Edge Flowers: Follow general directions on pages 58-67.

Follow these additional techniques and suggested embellishments unique to this Flower.

Making Ribbon Sepals

1. Cut 12" ribbon into four 3" pieces.

2. Fold, and stitch across bottom edge. Tack middle.

3. Slip under petals. Do not press Sepals.

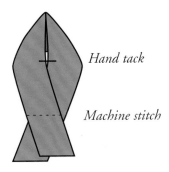

Hand tack

Machine stitch

4. You can also substitute ribbon with 1" long pieces of ½" or ¾" wide rickrack for Sepals.

"Fussy cut" the center and sew beads around the outside edge. A textured fabric was used for Leaves.

Satin stitch a center circle with radiating lines.

Sew four bugle beads and one glass bead in center.

Arrowhead

Arrowhead Added to Magic Vine Quilt

our nice new quilt. The stamens of this Flower are a soft orange shading into yellow. I suggest a fast color calico or English print for the round center which looks something like the ice cream in a cone.

"The triangular Flower with its two petals showing is of the pale pink, also of fast color gingham."

She really should have used a triangular-shaped leaf with this plantain, but since the vine is the magic one which never grew on land or sea, she designed the same leaves for all parts of the vine, no matter what the Flowers might be.

At the base of the Arrowhead Flower vine you can see a dotted line which indicates where next week's leaf will be appliqued. The leaf may always be made ahead of time, since it is always cut from the same pattern applied first in one slanting direction and then in the other.

A duplicate of this block was made for the third strip which would make up the series of four in the finished quilt.

The first and third strips are duplicates; the second and fourth strips are alike.

Copyright, 1930

In making the quilt, the Nancy Page Neighborhood Club found that they would have to brush up on wild Flowers and those which were better known in grandmother's day than in their own. Few of the members had ever heard of the Flower called Arrowhead and yet Nancy assured them it was well-known in the woods near her childhood home.

"This Flower," began Nancy, "is a member of the water plantain family. It is usually white in color but I have seen it in that misty, film, baby pink for our second quilt block in this Magic Vine.

"Evening Primrose in pale yellow and Arrowhead in pale pink can well grow on this vine that-never-was but soon-will-be in

1. Optional: Photocopy page and place on light table.

2. Place 7½" Background square on Placement Page.

3. Trace Stem line.

4. Cut 4½" long bias Stem and sew to Background square with your chosen method.

Yardage and Patterns

Cut one set for each block.

Triangular Petals
Baby Pink
4" square

Stamens
Orange Yellow
2½" square

Leaves and Stem
Green
3½" x 4"
4½" bias

Overlapping Leaf
Green
2" x 3"

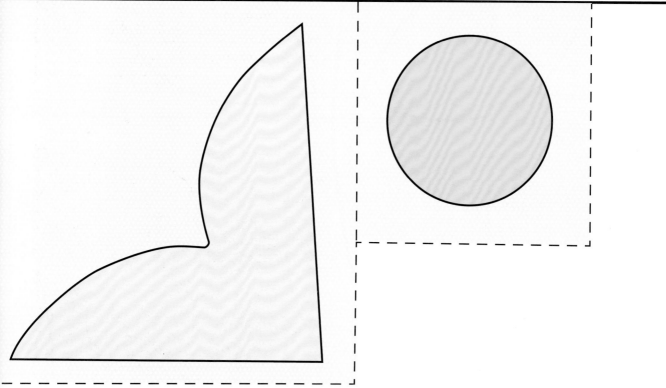

Quick Turn Flowers: Follow general directions on pages 36-57.
Raw Edge Flowers: Follow general directions on pages 58-67.

Follow these additional techniques and suggested embellishments unique to this Flower.

Quick Turn Flower

1. When sewing around Flower, take one straight stitch across V so Flower turns.

2. Clip to stitches before turning right side out.

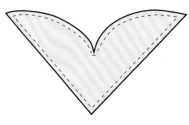

Raw Edge Flower

1. Notice how there are no stitches inside V. Satin stitch into V, pivot with needle down on outside edge, and continue stitching.

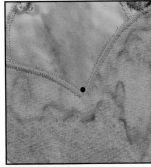

•*Pivot points*

2. At outside corners, stitch to the end, and stop with needle down on outside edge. Pivot, and continue stitching on next side.

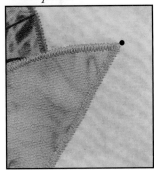

Stem stitch three lines with yellow floss, and stitch French Knots on ends.

Fussy cut fabric for Stamens, and embellish it with large seed beads.

Phlox

Phlox Is Newest Blossom on Magic Vine Quilt

no attention to the leaves which belonged with any one Flower but chose a leaf pattern which repeated itself over and over.

The leaves of the whole vine in this strip are of dark green. The joining leaf which puts two blocks together and gives the vine continuity is a light shade of green.

They seamed or stitched it to the finished second block which had the Arrowhead Flower given last week. This gave them three white blocks in a strip. The first one had the Evening Primrose, the second one the Arrowhead and now they were ready for the Phlox.

Now, using one of those joining leaves, pin it in place under the Phlox petal of this block. It will eventually go over the vine or stem of the Arrowhead block.

Note that its slant is reversed from that used in putting the Evening Primrose and Arrowhead blocks together. In other words this leaf slants just the opposite way.

Remember that this joining leaf is made of the lighter shade of green. After the joining leaf is in place pin the Flower and leaves as indicated in the small insert.

These blocks are repeated for the third vine strip down the quilt, so it is wise to make two of them while you have the patterns at hand.

Copyright, 1930

When Nancy brought out the pattern for the third block in the Magic Vine Quilt there was a general exclamation from all the neighborhood club members. "Oh, I know that one – it's Phlox! We used to have it in our garden at home. And in the Phlox bed we had pale pink, pink and white, a lavender Phlox and even a soft yellow."

"I know," said Nancy, "that's why I chose this Flower, because you can use almost any color. I thought you might have a scrap of fast color material left from one of your summer dresses and here would be the very place to put it."

Once more Nancy mentioned the fact that this magic vine paid

Placement Page

1. Optional: Photocopy page and place on light table.

2. Place 7½" Background square on Placement Page.

3. Trace Stem line.

4. Cut 4" long bias Stem and sew to Background square with your chosen method.

Yardage and Patterns

Petals
Lavender
4½" square

Center
Dark Purple Embroidery
Floss and Beads or
1½" square

Leaves and Stem
Green
3½" x 4"
4" bias

Overlapping Leaf
Green
2" x 3"

Cut one set for each block.

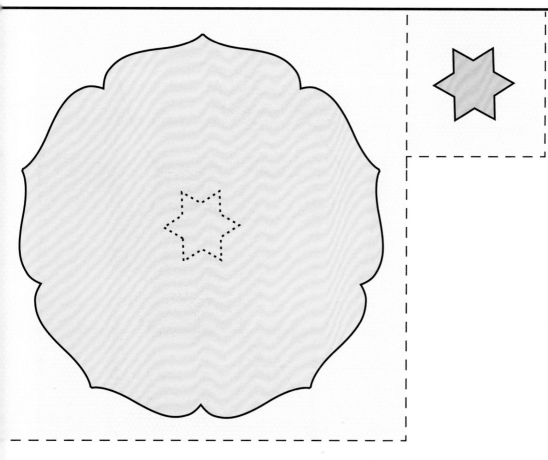

78

Quick Turn Flowers: Follow general directions on pages 36-57.
Raw Edge Flowers: Follow general directions on pages 58-67.

Follow these additional techniques and suggested embellishments unique to this Flower.

Raw Edge Flower Finished with Satin Stitch

1. Divide Phlox into five petals with satin stitch.

2. Cover ends of thread with satin stitch around the outside edge.

3. At outside point, stitch to the end, and stop with needle down on outside edge. Pivot, and continue stitching on next side.

4. Satin stitch around Star made with black fabric.

5. Embellish with beads.

Embellish with one 4mm glass bead in the center, surrounded by six 4mm darker faceted beads.

79

Trillium

Magic Vine Quilt Adds a Soft Purple Trillium

"Do you know, Nancy," said one, "I believe this is going to be as pretty as the basket quilt. I never thought anything could equal that, but really this Magic Vine is blossoming into a thing of rare beauty."

Nancy glowed with pleasure. She did think that the four trailing vines which would make up the center part of the quilt would be attractive with their wealth of pastel colored Flowers, their soft green leaves and wavy stem.

Then she liked to think of these vines against the white background and bordered with the soft green and white vine that encircled them almost like a wreath.

This Wake Robin or Trillium used soft purple with a reddish hue, soft green sepals and sturdy green leaves.

The little center circle of soft orange is applied over the purple. Since the quilt has four strips of vines and since the first and third are of the same pattern it is wise to make a second Trillium block while the patterns are still at hand.

At least, this is what the club members did.

Copyright, 1930

In the Grandmother's Garden Quilt which the Nancy Page neighborhood club had made a year or so ago the Trillium was one of the most popular blocks. That was one reason why Nancy planned to use it in this new Magic Vine Quilt. Surely no vine that ever grew could produce Evening Primroses, Phlox and Trilliums on the same parent stem, but then this Magic Vine grew in Never-Never-Land where dreams come true and things of beauty are everywhere about. And weren't the club members growing enthusiastic about this new quilt!

1. Optional: Photocopy page and place on light table.

2. Place 7½" Background square on Placement Page.

3. Trace Stem line.

4. Cut 4½" long bias Stem and sew to Background square with your chosen method.

Yardage and Patterns

Cut one set for each block.

 Petals
Reddish Purple or White
4½" square

 Sepals
Accent Green
1½" x 3½"

 Center
Yellow Embroidery Floss
and Beads

 Leaves and Stem
Green
3½" x 4"
4½" bias

 Overlapping Leaf
Green
2" x 3"

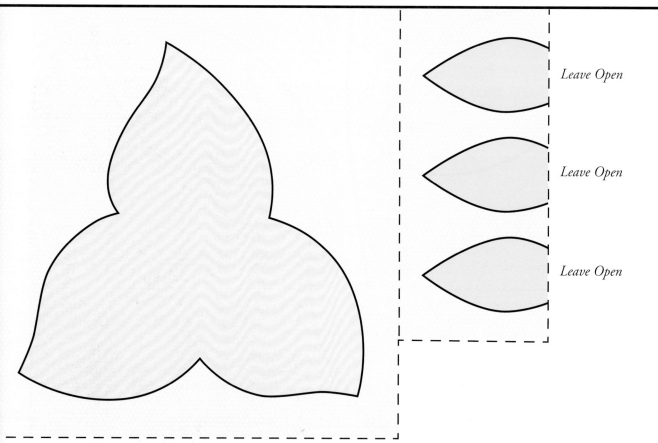

Leave Open

Leave Open

Leave Open

Quick Turn Flowers: Follow general directions on pages 36-57.
Raw Edge Flowers: Follow general directions on pages 58-67.

Follow these additional techniques and suggested embellishments unique to this Flower.

Quick Turn Flower

1. Divide Trillium into three parts by hand with backstitch and #5 pearl cotton.

2. Hand sew French Knots in center.

3. Sew tiny stitches radiating out from center.

Raw Edge Flower Finished with Satin Stitch

1. Fuse and satin stitch Sepals before fusing Flower. Stitch only points of Sepals.

2. Starting in center, divide Trillium into three parts with satin stitch.

3. For circle, place thread spool on fabric and trace.

4. If stitches don't cover edges, sew over it a second time with wider stitch width.

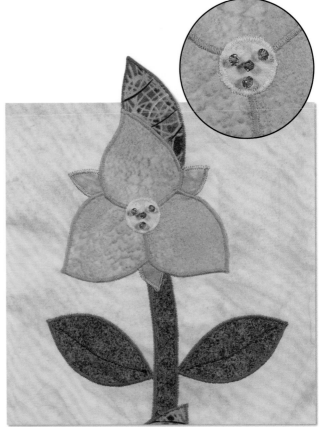

A striped fabric was used for Sepals and one leaf to give Flower more dimension.

Embellish center circle with 5mm glass beads.

Blue Eyed Grass

Quaint Blue Blossom is Added to Magic Vine

It was great fun to watch the Magic Vine grow and blossom. The first four Flowers had been just about the prettiest ever seen, according to the members of the club. One of the group had raised the question as to whether the third long vine should be an exact duplication of the first vine. "We might use the same Flowers, don't you know, but work them out in different colors." The club was about evenly divided as to the wisdom of this.

"You know in the old-fashioned quilts which our grandmothers made, much of the beauty lay in the repetition and more or less geometrical pattern. If we make the Flowers different colors in all four vines aren't we going to lose some of the beauty and simplicity which would come from repetition?" Such was the argument of the other side. Finally the group did the sensible thing and agreed to let each person work out her own idea. But in all cases the patterns for the third and first lengthwise vine were identical. The second and fourth vines grew the same Flowers, which differed of course from the first and third.

The Flower chosen for the next blossom on the Magic Vine was a member of the orchid family. It is called "Blue-Eyed Grass." The color should be blue, not too deep or strong a blue. The center should be of pale yellow, or of white. As Nancy said, one would never think of having such a Flower growing on a fat and chubby stem. It belongs on a reedy, grass-like stem, but since this is the vine that never, never grew it is quite permissible to put the starry blossom on the Magic Vine.

The petal patterns are alike, so that one petal will serve for the five. After Nancy had designed this pattern she discovered that the Blue-Eyed Grass had six petals. She told the members that they might add a sixth petal by overlapping the original five. That proved easy for the experienced needle workers.

The thorn-like points were worked with fast color blue embroidery cotton. The dotted lines at the top of the Flower indicate the overlapping leaf which is put in place when the Trillium block and this one have been seamed or pieced together.

Copyright, 1930

84

1. Optional: Photocopy page and place on light table.

2. Place 7½" Background square on Placement Page.

3. Trace Stem line.

4. Cut 4¼" long bias Stem and sew to Background square with your chosen method.

Yardage and Patterns

Cut one set for each block.

Petals
Blue
2½" x 7"

2½" x 4¾"

Center
1¾" square or
Yellow Embroidery Floss
or Beads

Thorn-like Points
Blue Embroidery Floss
or Blue Thread

Leaves and Stem
Green
3½" x 4"
4¼" bias

Overlapping Leaf
Green
2" x 3"

Quick Turn Flowers: Follow general directions on pages 36-57.

Raw Edge Flowers: Follow general directions on pages 58-67.

Follow these additional techniques and suggested embellishments unique to this Flower.

Stitching Center and Thorns

1. Embellish center with a button, beads, or embroidery floss stitched into French Knots. If you make French Knots, trace the star first and then fill it.

2. For thorns by hand, make a pointed stain stitch.

3. For thorns by machine, select a decorative stitch that resembles a thorn. Stitch beginning with widest part on the inside, and stitch out to the point until stitch is completed. You could also use a zigzag stitch. Begin wide and reduce width into point.

Raw Edge Flower

1. To cover ends, fuse and sew #1 Petal first.

2. Fuse and sew #2 and #3 next.

3. Fuse and sew #4 and #5 last.

4. Cover center with Star and beads.

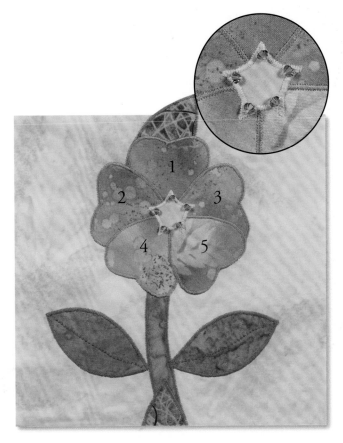

To select desired texture, divide out parts of fabric with fingers. Sew three glass beads in center.

Milkwort

Still Another Blossom for the Magic Vine Quilt

One effect of the work on the Magic Vine was to send the club members scurrying to their Flower guide books and their botanies. They discovered that many a common, every-day Flower seemed a stranger only when they heard of it by name. Take the Milkwort, for instance. Most of them had seen this small Flower which grew low from a fleshy stem and from a base, seemingly, of broad, bright green leaves. These leaves turn a bronze red in the winter.

When the club members gathered for this meeting, they had great tales to tell of the way in which their quilts were being admired. One member said that her sorority had asked her to make one for the sorority house in the nearby university. It was wanted to add the finishing touch to the guest room. Martha said that her church was waiting week by week for the patterns. The "Ladies Aid" were planning on having the quilt for the next bazaar.

Josephine said she was making it for her guest room. Martha replied that any quilt on which she put as much work as this was going right into her own bedroom, where she could see it daily and admire her own handiwork. Lois was making her's for her baby daughter, Ann. She was already visioning it in her daughter's hope chest.

All of this the group chattered over as they worked. For the Milkwort they choose a piece of rather deep, but soft, pink material. It was color fast, as were all the pieces chosen for the quilt. When the members were in doubt they washed a sample of the material to see how it laundered.

There were two petals of the Flower, cut in one piece, a small rounded piece, called the pouch. This terminated in antlers which are shown here as a solid pie-shaped piece. They might well be made of fast color embroidery cotton in yellow.

Remember that this Flower is duplicated in the third long vine, so be sure to make two Milkwort blocks.

1. Optional: Photocopy page
   and place on light table.

2. Place 7½" Background square
   on Placement Page.

3. Trace Stem line.

4. Cut 4" long bias Stem and sew to Background square with your chosen method.

Yardage and Patterns

Petals
Deep Pink
4" x 5¾"

Pouch
Pink
1½" x 2½"

Antlers
Pink
Embroidery Floss

Leaves and Stem
Green
3½" x 4"
4" bias

Overlapping Leaf
Green
2" x 3"

Cut one set for each block.

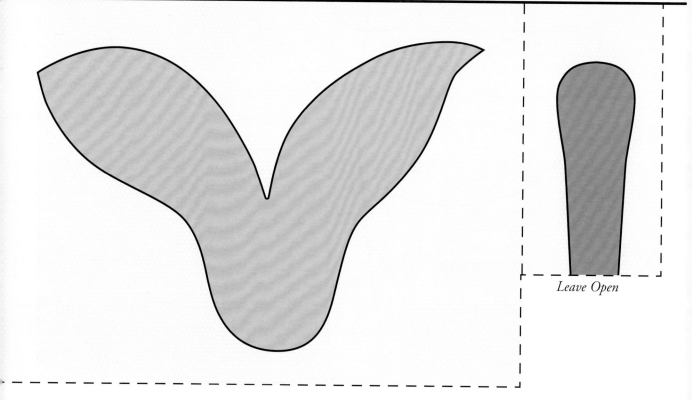

Leave Open

90

Quick Turn Flowers: Follow general directions on pages 36-57.
Raw Edge Flowers: Follow general directions on pages 58-67.

Follow these additional techniques and suggested embellishments unique to this Flower.

Loop Stitching

1. Sew pouch and Petals in place.

2. Cut off three strands of embroidery floss or rayon thread 22" long, knot end, and bring thread up from wrong side to edge of pouch.

3. Make a 1" loop, hold onto it, and put needle back down close to where needle entered, each time holding loops.

4. Go in and out, make about six loops.

5. Knot on back.

6. Cut loops, and trim to desired length.

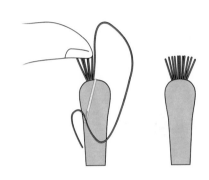

Quick Turn Milkwort

Raw Edge Milkwort

Compare the two Flower versions. The Raw Edge Milkwort is a mirror image of the Quick Turn Milkwort. It is hardly noticeable with most of the Magic Vine Flowers.

Downy Gentian

Magic Vine Quilt Adds A Violet Blue Gentian

Margaret was one of the members of the Needlework Club who was quite a botanist. She recognized most of the Flowers which Nancy designed for the Magic Vine Quilt. That was a tribute to Nancy's skill as an artist, for it is quite true that many of her Flowers could not be found, just as she drew them, on hill or vale, in meadow or in woodland. But that did not mean that they were not effective when they were translated into a quilt pattern for the Magic Vine.

Some one asked a club member where they ever got the name "Magic Vine." "Well, you see, it is like this — we have a vine that never could have grown, for on it there are Flowers of spring, of summer and late fall. It is a vine that grows in Never-Never Land where orchids and dandelions are as friendly as the lion and the lamb. It is in truth, a Magic Vine."

The light block in the quilt series was the gentian, that Flower that has poems written in tribute to it. The Gentian, at least the downy one is not as fringed as the other Gentian, even though it belongs to the same family. But it does have some of the same quality of blue in its coloring. The Flowers are violet blue, soft and dainty enough to have deserved the adjective — downy.

Nancy suggested that the members use two shades of violet blue in developing this Flower, making the fore part of the Flower a lighter shade than the part in the background. The leaves are green, so are the stem and the tiny leaves at the base of the Flower. Even though the stem and base are in one piece, Nancy strongly advised making the stem in the usual fashion and then appliqueing the whorl of leaves at the base of the Flower.

Nancy announced that the next Flower had three initials, F. B. D. and challenged the group to guess what it would be.

1. Optional: Photocopy page and place on light table.

2. Place 7½" Background square on Placement Page.

3. Trace Stem line.

4. Cut 4" long bias Stem and sew to Background square with your chosen method.

Yardage and Patterns

Front Petals
Light Violet Blue
4" x 5¾"

Back Petals
Dark Violet Blue
2½" x 4"

Base of Flower
Green
1¾" x 2½"

Leaves and Stem
Green
3½" x 4"
4" bias

Overlapping Leaf
Green
2" x 3"

Cut one set for each block.

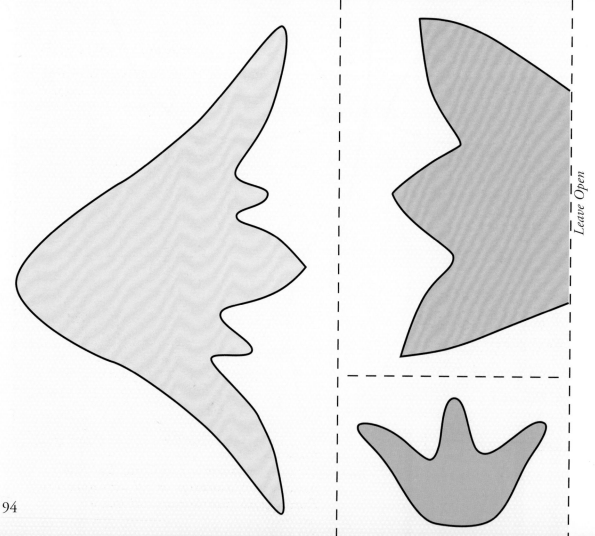

Leave Open

Quick Turn Flowers: Follow general directions on pages 36-57.

Raw Edge Flowers: Follow general directions on pages 58-67.

Follow these additional techniques and suggested embellishments unique to this Flower.

Repair a hole with Roxanne's Glue-Baste-It.

Place a tiny drop of glue in area to be repaired.

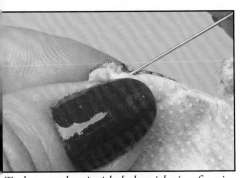

Tuck raw edges inside hole with tip of a pin.

Let Flower dry.

Quick Turn Flower – Repairing a Tear

1. If you accidentally poke a hole in the edge of your Flower while turning it right side out, it can be repaired.

2. Use Roxanne's Glue Baste-It® for the repair. Keep little white cap on the bottle when not in use.

3. Remove white cap, and replace it with nozzle tip. From right side, place a tiny, controlled dot of glue in area to be repaired.

4. Tuck raw edges inside the hole with tip of a pin.

5. Let Flower dry.

6. Replace white cap. Immediately soak the nozzle tip in a cup of warm water. Continue cleaning by slipping a large pin in and out of the nozzle.

Quick Turn Flower
Use a very small straw to turn Leaf at Base. From inside, carefully push out point with sharp point turner. From right side, pick out points with stiletto.

False Beech Drop

Old-Fashioned Calico Flowers for Magic Vine Quilt

"All right, Nance, we'll let you off this time, but why do they call it a False Beech Drop?" "Oh, I can explain that," chimed in Judy. "There is a real beech drop, a sort of fleshy parasitical thing which grows near beech roots. This particular Flower grows near the roots of oaks and pines. Because its shape is similar to that of the real beech drop it is given that name, but because it favors oaks it is called a false drop.

Nancy told them the Flower was a crimson red, lightly touched with yellow.

This made the group think they might use some of the old fashioned dotted calicoes or the copies of the Flowered calico, which has a red ground with an all-over pattern in small yellow Flowers.

Remember that this Flower is repeated in the third long vine which is in the quilt. That means that two blocks with the beech drop will be made.

The club members were so interested in guessing the Flower to come that Nancy gave them a little peek at the next Flower. You can see it in the corner of today's pattern. Guess what it will be. It's initials are B. B.

Copyright, 1930

The club members came with anticipation. They had been told by Nancy that the new Flower would have the initials F. B. D. They had searched Flower guide books in vain. One member, Judy, said she had the name, but that Nancy's Flower did not resemble her Flower.

"I think it is a False Beech Drop, but if I am right then the Flowers ought not to be so upstanding; they ought to droop more than you have them doing."

"Oh dear, Judy, you are too literal. This is the False Beech Drop, but I could not make the blossoms droop because it would have spoiled the symmetry of the vine. So I just pretended that the Flowers stood upright when they grew on the Magic Vine Quilt. Anyway, you know this vine thrives in Never-Never Land, so I think I am safe."

1. Optional: Photocopy page and place on light table.

2. Place 7½" Background square on Placement Page.

3. Trace Stem line.

4. Cut 4" long bias Stem and sew to Background square with your chosen method.

Yardage and Patterns

First Flower
Crimson Red with Yellow
3" x 4"

Second Flower
Different Red
3" x 4"

Leaves and Stem
Green
3½" x 4"
4" bias

Overlapping Leaf
Green
2" x 3"

Cut one set for each block.

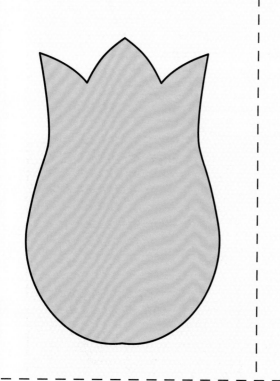

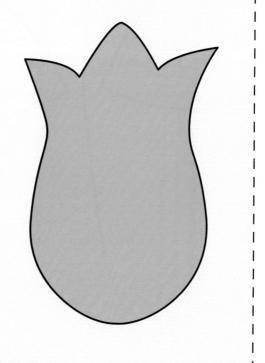

Quick Turn Flowers: Follow general directions on pages 36-57.
Raw Edge Flowers: Follow general directions on pages 58-67.

Follow these additional techniques and suggested embellishments unique to this Flower.

False Beech Drop has been mistaken for the Tulip block. But as Nancy explained, if the Flowers droop like a real False Beech Drop, it would have spoiled the symmetry in the vine.

1. "Fussy cut" darker part of fabric on upper part of Flower to represent shade.

2. The two Flowers are very close in size. Place smaller Flower underneath front flower.

As Nancy suggested, old fashioned dotted calicos were used for this False Beech Drop.

For a contemporary look, fabric with yellow mottled on crimson red was used.

Sew pieces in order.

99

Bouncing Bet

Bouncing Bet New Addition to Magic Vine

This was the story that Nancy told when the quilt club members met to make the ninth Flower in the Magic Vine Quilt. This Magic Vine which grows in only one place, Never-Never Land, has Flowers of every shape and hue growing from its stem. Nancy knew that Magic Vines were springing up all over the country, judging from the interest women were showing in her quilt. She knew too that before long these vines would flourish in many a bedroom from Maine to California. This again proved that the vine was a magic one, since climate, distance and season affected it not at all.

The Flower in this Bouncing Bet may well be a piece of fast color, figured pink and white print. This material has been immensely popular for dresses during the past Summer and almost every woman will find a scrap or two in her piece bag. The center is pale yellow. The leaves and stem are dark green. The over-lapping leaves indicated by the dotted lines at the top and bottom of the pattern are cut from material of a lighter shade of green. The upper one is put in place before the Flower is appliqued. The final stitching of the leaf is delayed until the block is finished. Then it overlaps the stem which joins this Bouncing Bet block to the False Beech Drop.

Nancy gave the members no hint as to the next Flower beyond saying that it was a gay and cheering morning Flower.

Copyright, 1930

"Once upon a time there was a country girl, all pink and white who never could keep still. She bounced from one thing to another from morning until night. Her name was Elizabeth, but her family called her 'Bet.' One day her father was out walking with her and saw a pink and white Flower that seemed alert and alive. It did not have the repose of the Easter Lily nor the pathos of the Pansy. When her father saw it, he said, 'do you know, I have a name for that Flower. It is just like you. I am going to call it Bouncing Bet'. And Bouncing Bet it has been to this day."

1. Optional: Photocopy page and place on light table.

2. Place 7½" Background square on Placement Page.

3. Trace Stem line.

4. Cut 3½" long bias Stem and sew to Background square with your chosen method.

Yardage and Patterns

 Petals
Pink and White
5¼" square

 Center
Pale Yellow
1½" square
or beads

 Leaves and Stem
Green
3½" x 4"
3½" bias

 Overlapping Leaf
Green
2" x 3"

Cut one set for each block.

102

Quick Turn Flowers: Follow general directions on pages 36-57.
Raw Edge Flowers: Follow general directions on pages 58-67.
Follow these additional techniques and suggested embellishments unique to this Flower.

Center for Flower

1. Trace ⅞" circle on template plastic and cut out.

2. Draw circle on center of turned Bouncing Bet, and outline by hand with stem stitch.

3. Satin stitch center. On any circle larger than ½", sew satin stitch with overlapping stitches. *Stitch only halfway, and make second stitch to edge. Stitches overlap and are not loose.*

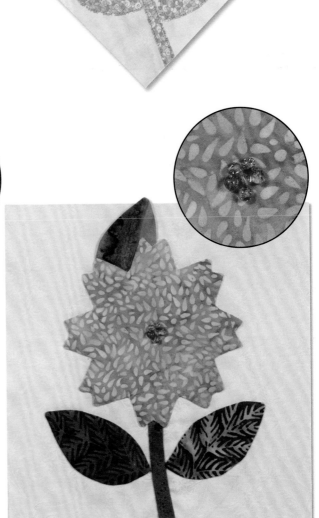

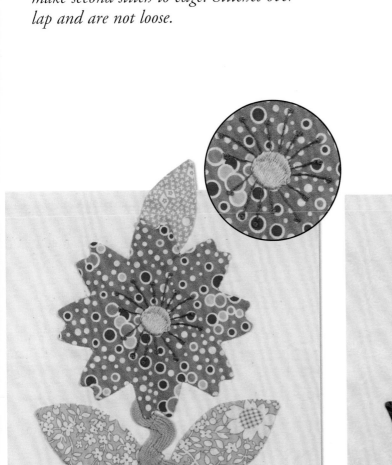

Stem stitch lines radiate from center, with French Knots on the ends of each line.

Beads add beauty and dimension to your Flower. Knot after sewing each bead for added strength.

Morning Glory

Morning Glory Adds Beauty to Magic Vine Quilt

color choices which the various members of the club picked out from their piece bags.

The Morning Glory in the first long vine is repeated in the third long vine so it is necessary to make the two quilt blocks with Morning Glory pattern.

Some of the Members wanted to bell the edges of the Morning Glory somewhat. A few wanted to indent or slightly scallop the edges so that a more irregular outline was secured.

The members now had just one more Flower to put on the Magic Vine which makes the first and third long ones in the quilt. There are eleven Flowers in each long vine. The first and third vines are duplicated. The second and fourth are duplicated.

All told there are twenty-two different Flowers growing on this Magic Vine that flourishes in Never-Never Land. The drift of pastel colors mingling with the soft green of the vine is fast becoming a thing of beauty. Everyone who saw the quilt when a Nancy Page Quilt Club member was working on it wanted to go right home and start one just like it. "I don't blame them, do you?" was Nancy's answer when this remark was passed on to her.

Copyright, 1930

Just as soon as the members saw the flaring blossom which was the pattern for the day they said, "Oh we know what this is, Nancy. It's a Morning Glory." And Morning Glory it was.

With a Flower as fragile and as colorful as the Morning Glory the color range was wide.

"Only," cautioned Nancy, "be sure that what ever material you choose is color fast. We don't want to spoil a quilt on which there is as much work as this by using some material with the colors that run when the quilt is washed. A dainty yellow and white material, a pink and white, soft lavender and blue are

1. Optional: Photocopy page
   and place on light table.

2. Place 7½" Background
   square on Placement Page.

3. Trace Stem line.

4. Cut 5" long bias Stem
   and sew to Background square with your chosen method.

Yardage and Patterns

Cut one set for each block.

 Flower
Lavender Blue
3½" x 4½"

 Scallop Edge
Deeper Lavender Blue
1¼" x 11"
or Ribbon
⅜" x 13"
or Rickrack
⅜" x 6"

 Leaves and Stem
Green
3½" x 4"
5" bias

 Overlapping Leaf
Green
2" x 3"

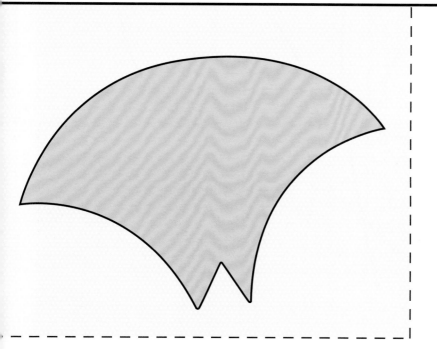

Quick Turn Flowers: Follow general directions on pages 36-57.
Raw Edge Flowers: Follow general directions on pages 58-67.

Follow these additional techniques and suggested embellishments unique to this Flower.

Scalloped Top Edge with Fabric

The scallop technique is referred to as Ruching.

1. Fold raw edges of 1¼" x 11" strip to center, wrong sides together. Press.

2. Place folded raw edges underneath.

3. Along top edge, begin 1" from right end, and make small dots on the edges every 1". Along bottom edge, begin ½" from right edge and make small dots every 1".

4. Thread a hand sewing needle with an 18" double strand of matching thread, and knot. Wax your thread so it doesn't tangle.

5. At the right end of the strip, turn edge under ½".

6. Beginning at turned under edge, stitch running stitches from dot to dot in zigzag direction. Loop the thread over the folded edge each time you change direction. Stitch several inches and pull, gathering the fabric on both sides.

7. Turn under the last ½" and stitch to the end, gathering to 5" to 5½". Adjust the petals to the same size as the top of the Morning Glory, and knot.

8. Hand stitch to top of Flower.

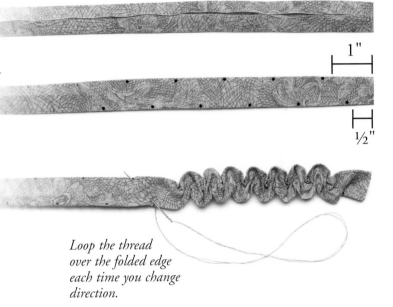

1"

½"

Loop the thread over the folded edge each time you change direction.

This ruching was made with ribbon.

As an alternative, hand stitch ⅜" x 6" rickrack to top of Morning Glory.

Wild Rose

Wild Rose Newest Blossom on Green Vine

Wild Rose Newest Blossom on Green Vine

be full of briers that scratch. "It does not look as though this rose would scratch. Isn't it attractive as Nancy has drawn it? What colors do you want us to use, Nancy?"

"Choose a pale pink for the blossoms. Have the centers worked in fast color embroidery cotton in yellow. You want green for the stem and leaves, of course.

"The leaf which joins this block onto its neighbor, the Morning Glory, is made of fast color green gingham in the lighter shade of green. There is no leaf at the bottom of this stem because this Flower is at the bottom of the first vine. When the rose is done then you have one magic vine with its 11 Flowers completed. This vine is repeated for the third vine. But when you come next week we start on the second Magic Vine which is repeated for the fourth strip."

"Call this Flower by any name you please, it still has a poetic significance. You may think of the sweet brier, the eglantine or the wild rose, but in every case there is some poem, some song or some romantic memory which is called to mind." It was Doris, the librarian member of the Nancy Page needlework club, who expressed herself, "Don't you recall that poem of Milton's, in which he calls to mind the eglantine, and as for sweetbrier, many and many a lad has likened the lady of his heart to a rose-sweet but inclined to

As the club members worked they asked one of their members to play MacDowells "To a Wild Rose." And Doris persisted in quoting poetry. So all in all they had quite an esthetic afternoon.

Copyright, 1930

1. Optional: Photocopy page and place on light table.

2. Place 7½" Background square on Placement Page.

3. Trace Stem line.

4. Cut 6" long bias Stem and sew to Background square with your chosen method.

Straight Set Blocks: If you are making Vines exactly as the Nancy Page Club members with eleven in each row, this is the last block in the first and third rows for Twin, Full/Queen and King plus fifth for King. It does not have an Overlapping Leaf at the bottom of Stem.

Yardage and Patterns

Cut one set for each block.

Petals
Pink
3¼" x 5"

Deeper Pink
3¼" x 5"

Centers
Yellow and Brown
Embroidery Floss
or #5 Pearl Cotton
Beads

Leaves and Stem
Green
3½" x 4"
6" bias

Overlapping Leaf
Green
2" x 3"

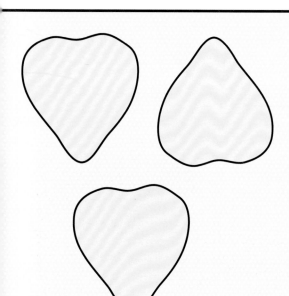

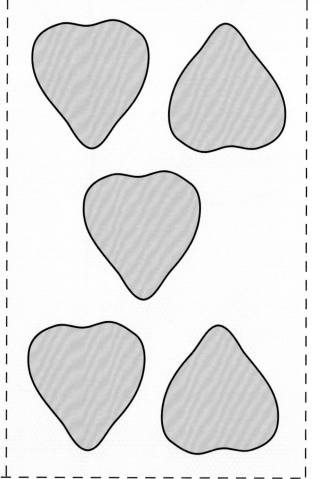

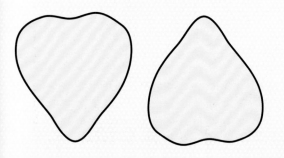

Quick Turn Flowers: Follow general directions on pages 36-57.
Raw Edge Flowers: Follow general directions on pages 58-67.

Follow these additional techniques and suggested embellishments unique to this Flower.

Quick Turn Flowers

1. Trace petals, sew on lines whole way around petal, and trim.

2. Clip small hole in interfacing and turn right side out with small straw and bodkin. *A small crochet hook can be substituted for a bodkin.*

3. Fuse in place.

4. Sew radiating stitches from center out, and finish with French Knots.

5. Sew beads in centers.

Raw Edge Flowers

1. Fuse all Petals in back Flower first, and stitch around outside edges. It's the red Flower in this example.

2. Fuse all Petals in front Flower next and stitch around edges.

3. Sew beads to centers.

Shooting Star

Quilters Start on Second and Fourth Magic Vines

It was quite an excited group who met for the Needlework Club gathering. They had finished one whole strip of the Magic Vine, repeated it for another strip which would later become the third long vine climbing up the new and beautiful Magic Vine Quilt.

They looked at the Primrose, the Arrowhead, Phlox and the Trillium. They exclaimed anew at the beauty of the Downy Gentian. Mary was loud in her praise of the Bouncing Bet. Doris sang the praises of the Wild Rose. Caroline chose the Morning Glory. In fact, it was hard to find a Flower which did not have its own adherents. Some of the members had spent the past week in piecing some of the vine which would later make a frame for the whole pattern. And now they were ready to start on the second long vine which would appear again as the fourth one in the finished quilt.

There are to be eleven Flowers which have not been found in the first vine. Nancy said that her husband, Peter, said he never had known of a vine which could grow eleven kinds of blossoms from one stem and root. And Nancy said, "This is a new kind of vine. It is a magic one which grows like a chameleon or rainbow. It has no rhyme nor reason, but it does have beauty." And Peter grunted "uh-huh, it sure has."

The first Flower in the vine is properly placed. It is a Shooting Star and shoots it's way up and up, aspiring to the heavens and the blue above.

The petals are reddish lavender and the anthers on the stamens are a rich gold. They are so shaped that they give the effect of a golden cone or center. Each Flower has five petals, all cut from the same pattern. But some of the petals overlap so that the finished effect is not monotonous.

In this vine the leaves and stem are made of a lighter shade of green. The leaf which joins two white blocks together, being appliqued in place after the blocks are stitched, is cut from dark green.

Repeat this Flower for the first block in the fourth long vine.

Copyright, 1930

1. Optional: Photocopy page and place on light table.

2. Place 7½" Background square on Placement Page.

3. Trace Stem line.

4. Cut 1¼" and 5" long bias Stems. Make 1¼" Stem slightly narrower and sew to Background square first. Cover raw edge with 5" Stem and sew to Background square with your chosen method.

Straight Set Blocks: If you are making vines exactly as the Nancy Page Club members with eleven in each row, this is the first block in the second and fourth rows for Twin, Full/Queen, and King. The first block in the row does <u>not</u> have an Overlapping Leaf at the top, but it does have one at the bottom.

Yardage and Patterns

 Top and Bottom Petals
Reddish Lavender
4½" x 7"

 Middle Petals
Yellow Pink
3" x 6½"

 Anthers
Rich Gold
2" x 4"

 Leaf and Stem
Green
3½" square
1¼" x 4½" bias

 **Optional
Overlapping Leaf**
Green
2" x 3"

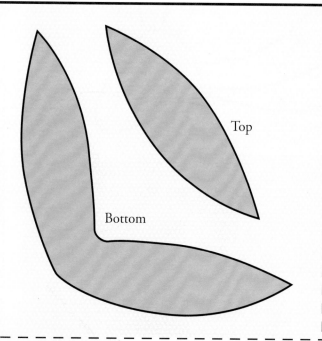

Top

Bottom

Middle

Trace twice for two Flowers.

Anther

Quick Turn Flowers: Follow general directions on pages 36-57.
Raw Edge Flowers: Follow general directions on pages 58-67.

Follow these additional techniques and suggested embellishments unique to this Flower.

Quick Turn Flowers

1. Make 1¼" Stem slightly narrower and sew to Background first.

2. Cover raw edge with 5" Stem, and sew to Background.

3. Trace, sew, trim and turn petals.

4. Place bottom petals on Background square.

5. Place middle petals second.

6. Place top petal next and anthers last.

7. Fuse in place, and stitch outside edges.

Optional: Stem stitch a connecting stem from lower Flower to main stem.

Raw Edge Flowers

1. Fuse and sew each piece individually from bottom, then middle, to top.

2. Fuse yellow anthers. If Flower color bleeds through, fuse a second yellow anthers on top.

Bottom petals

Middle petals

Top petals

Like the original Nancy page quilt, this is the top block in the second and fourth rows without Overlapping Leaf on top. It does have one at the bottom, however.

Poppy

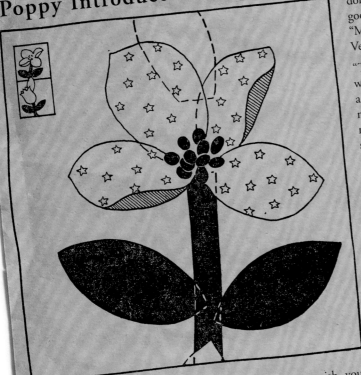

Poppy Introduces New Idea to Magic Vine Quilt

don't. I trust Nancy to do a good job all the way through." "Me too," chorused the group as Vera voiced her generous praise.

"Thanks a lot. Let's get to work on the Poppy for here we are doing something we have not done before – turning the material over for part of a petal, so that we get both wrong and right side showing in the same Flower." The members stopped talking and set to work.

The leaves and stem are made from the lighter shade of green and the connection leaf indicated here by the dotted line is cut from the darker shade. This reverses the colors used in the first and third vines. For the Poppy itself some of the members chose pale yellow, some rich orange, others pink.

"Do you know what I think, Nancy? I do believe that the second vine is going to be prettier than the first one. I love the Flower we are making today – the Poppy and the Shooting Star which we made last week was as pretty a Flower as ever I have seen."

"Oh, I don't agree with you, Jane." This from Lois. "I like that first vine with its Wild Rose and Trilliums and Bouncing Bet. Of course, I think these Poppies are lovely, but still –

"You are going to like the two vines equally when we are through, girls. You see if you

The center of the Poppy was worked in satin stitch with fast color embroidery cotton. Dark colors were used.

A second Poppy block is made for the fourth vine which is a duplicate of the second vine.

1. Optional: Photocopy page and place on light table.

2. Place 7½" Background square on Placement Page.

3. Trace Stem line.

4. Cut 5½" long bias Stem and sew to Background square with your chosen method.

Yardage and Patterns

Cut one set for each block.

 Top Petals
Orange
3¾" x 8½"

 Underneath Petals
Deeper Yellow
3¾" x 8½"

 Center
Orange
Embroidery Floss
or Beads

 Leaves and Stem
Green
3½" x 4"
5½" bias

 Overlapping Leaf
Green
2" x 3"

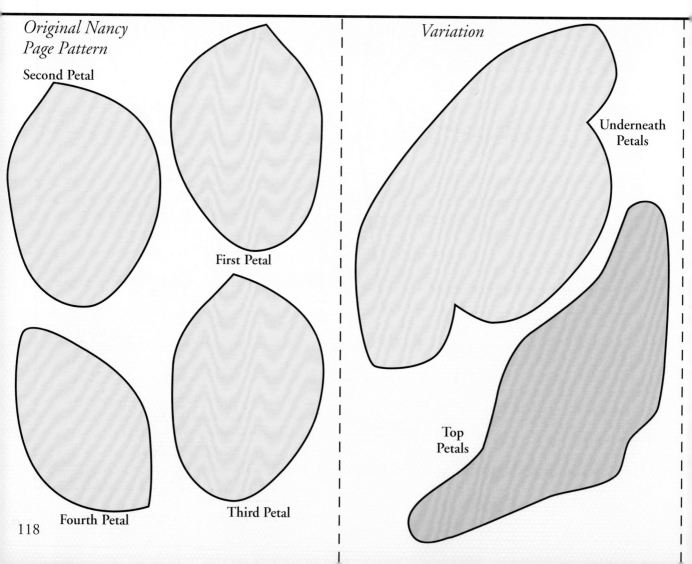

Original Nancy Page Pattern

Second Petal

First Petal

Fourth Petal

Third Petal

Variation

Underneath Petals

Top Petals

Quick Turn Flowers: Follow general directions on pages 36-57.
Raw Edge Flowers: Follow general directions on pages 58-67.

Follow these additional techniques and suggested embellishments unique to this Flower.

Quick Turn Flower for Original Nancy Page Poppy

1. Trace petals on template plastic, and cut out.

2. Place 3¾" x 8½" fabrics right sides together with underneath fabric on top.

3. Trace petals on underneath fabric, sew on lines, and trim ⅛" away. On first and third petals, cut small hole on wrong side of underneath fabric, and turn right side out.

4. Place Background square on Placement Page and pin petals in place, turning edges up on first and third petals. Sew turned edges in place.

5. Satin stitch seeds in center with embroidery floss, or sew bead in center.

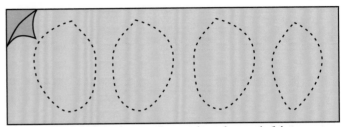

Place fabrics right sides together with underneath fabric on top.

Cut small holes on wrong side of underneath fabric.

Raw Edge Flower

1. Photocopy with mirror image feature on copier so flowers are placed the same as on Placement Page.

2. If you don't have a photocopier, turn pattern page over so printing is on bottom, and trace.

3. Do not mirror image Placement Page.

Place petals on Background in numbered order.

Poppy Variation

1. Make two pieces with chosen method.

2. Place Underneath Petals on Background, and sew in place.

3. Overlap Top Petals, and sew in place.

4. Back stitch lines with pearl cotton.

5. Optional: Stitch five beads in center.

Poppy Variation
Fussy cut fabric to represent shading on Flower.

Tulip

Pastel or Fine Print Tulips for Magic Vine Quilt

give thanks instead for the smooth edges of the every day Tulip."

"I guess you are right. Anyway, you have a pretty tulip there." So said the whole club.

Some of the members made the Tulip a pale yellow. Others chose a rosy pink. One member made hers a soft lavender. Some chose finely figured material as indicated in the drawing, others chose plain material in solid colors. The dark points were made of the same general kind of material as the large front part. But usually the color was darker. For instance, the pale yellow tulip had a deeper yellow for the back of the Tulip. The lavender used a purple for the darker portion and the pinky one used a rose. A second Tulip block was made for the fourth vine.

Some of the members tried using yellow for the Tulip in the second vine and a lavender for the Tulip in the fourth vine. But the general feeling was this: the quilt would look prettier when finished if the second and fourth vines were alike in coloring as well as in Flowers. But that is a matter of individual choice.

Great excitement reigned when the members saw the newest block for the Magic Vine Quilt. "I was hoping you would have a Tulip. Only I wish you had made it a Parrot Tulip, Nancy." "You try to applique the ragged edges of a Parrot Tulip, Marge, and you will never ask for it again, but

Copyright, 1930

Placement Page

1. Optional: Photocopy page and place on light table.

2. Place 7½" Background square on Placement Page.

3. Trace Stem line.

4. Cut 4" long bias Stem and sew to Background square with your chosen method.

Yardage and Patterns

Cut one set for each block.

 Flower
Yellow
3" x 4"

 Points
Yellow
1¼" x 3"

 Leaves and Stem
Green
3½" x 4"
4" bias

 Overlapping Leaf
Green
2" x 3"

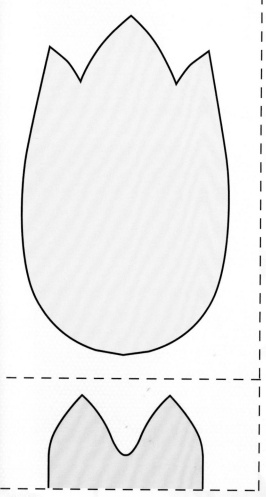

Leave Open

Quick Turn Flowers: Follow general directions on pages 36-57.

Raw Edge Flowers: Follow general directions on pages 58-67.

Follow these additional techniques and suggested embellishments unique to this Flower.

Quick Turn Flowers

1. Leave points open at bottom for turning.

2. Stem stitch lines with pearl cotton.

Raw Edge Flowers

1. If green Stem shows through light yellow tulip, cut second yellow tulip and fuse it on top.

2. Stitch around outside edge with a wider satin stitch.

Back stitch dimensional lines on Tulip before fusing it in place.

Embellish three points with glass beads.

Cosmos

Cosmos in Pink or Lavender for Magic Vine Quilt

"The other night I was working at my Magic Vine Quilt and a neighbor saw it. She was so enthusiastic about it. 'Can I start one now?' she asked. I told her that she could get the back patterns for 10 cents each. And she is going to start one at once. Then she wanted to know what other Flowers there were going to be in the quilt. I told her we never knew from week to week just what the next pattern would be. I told her that made the quilt so much more exciting. She looked at all the Flowers we had made. 'I don't see the Cosmos anywhere,' said she. And here we are with the Cosmos this week. I bet she'll think I have a 'drag' with you and asked you to put her Flower in."

Maybe it was thought transference, Jane. Maybe I felt her thought and unconsciously designed a Cosmos. But at any rate, here it is, and I think it's pretty. "How about the rest of you?" And the rest of them agreed that the block would be one of the prettiest they had made thus far.

All of the Cosmos petals are the same shape and size so that one pattern will do for them all.

In making the Cosmos the members used either soft pink or a soft lavender. Those members who made the Tulip lavender chose the pink Cosmos. And those who had chosen a yellow Tulip decided they could make their Cosmos either pink or lavender. A duplicate of this block is made for the fourth vine.

Copyright, 1930

124

Placement Page

1. Optional: Photocopy page and place on light table.

2. Place 7½" Background square on Placement Page.

3. Trace Stem line.

4. Cut 3½" long bias Stem and sew to Background square with your chosen method.

Yardage and Patterns

Cut one set for each block.

 Petals
Medium Pink
4¾" x 7"

 Center
Yellow
2½" Circle
or 1" button

 Leaves and Stem
Green
3½" x 4"
3½" bias

 Overlapping Leaf
Green
2" x 3"

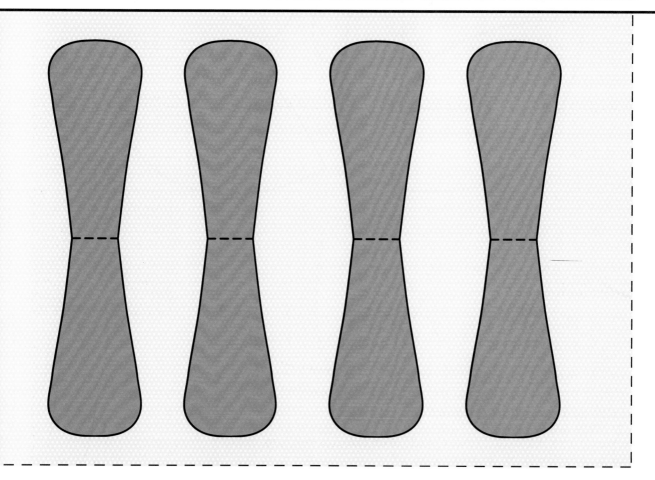

Quick Turn Flowers: Follow general directions on pages 36-57.
Raw Edge Flowers: Follow general directions on pages 58-67.

Follow these additional techniques and suggested embellishments unique to this Flower.

Quick Turn Flowers

1. Trace shapes, and sew around outside edges. Trim, cut in half on dashed lines, and turn right side out with thin straw and bodkin.

2. Gather ends into center and pull tight so there is a circular opening approximately ⅜".

3. Cover center with a yo-yo or button.

Raw Edge Flowers

1. Cut in half on dashed line for placement.

2. Fuse and sew in two stages.

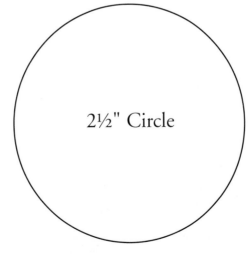

Making 1" Yo-Yo

1. Make 2½" circle template and trace on fabric. Cut out.

2. Thread a hand sewing needle with a double strand of matching thread, and knot.

3. Pull thread through Thread Heaven® so thread doesn't tangle.

4. From the wrong side, turn under the raw edge ¼" and run a long gathering stitch near the folded edge.

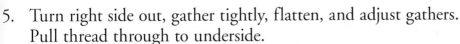

2½" Circle

5. Turn right side out, gather tightly, flatten, and adjust gathers. Pull thread through to underside.

6. Sew yo-yo to center of Flower with attached thread, and knot on back.

Bluebell

Bluebell Interesting Addition to Magic Vine Quilt

When the Needlework Club began to work on the Bluebell design they understood why Nancy had asked them to come to club meeting prepared to tell a Scotch story. And such a host of stories as there were! And how they laughed at the stories, and agreed that the stories were a myth, for each member had some incident which told of the kindness of a Scottish friend or neighbor.

They really did not believe that the Scots were pictured truly even though they were recalled Burns' lines which asked for some power "to see oursel's as ithers see us."

But after the stories were told and the daughter of the house had played "The Blue Bells of Scotland" with variations they settled to work.

There was no doubt as to the color of the Flower. It was blue, a soft blue which blended well with the rosy or lavender Cosmos in the block above. The longer the members worked at these quilts the more they appreciated the part which soft pastel colors played in the beauty of the finished quilt. A harsh crude color may have been used in the quilt made by grandmother but rooms of today call for the softer, quieter colors.

The very center of the Bluebell was worked in satin stitch with fast color embroidery cotton in yellow.

The two light points of the partially opened Bluebell were made of lighter colored material than was used for the main part of the Flower.

A duplicate of this block was made for the fourth vine.

Copyright, 1930

1. Optional: Photocopy page and place on light table.

2. Place 7½" Background square on Placement Page.

3. Trace Stem lines.

4. Cut 1¼" and 4½" long bias Stems. Make 1¼" Stem slightly narrower and sew to Background square first. Cover raw edge with 4½" Stem.

Yardage and Patterns

Cut one set for each block.

Flower
Lavender Blue
3½" square

Points and Flower
Blue
1½" x 3"
4" square

Leaves and Stem
Green
3½" x 4"
1¼" and 4½" bias

Overlapping Leaf
Green
2" x 3"

Center Circle
Yellow Embroidery Floss
or Beads

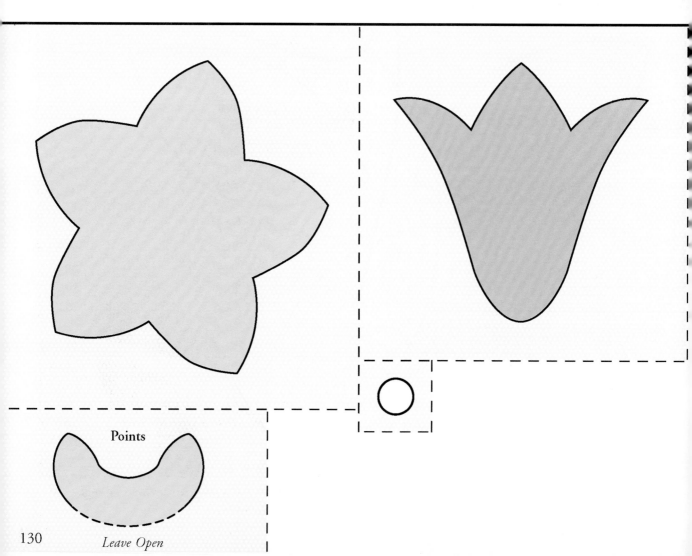

Points

Leave Open

130

Quick Turn Flowers: Follow general directions on pages 36-57.
Raw Edge Flowers: Follow general directions on pages 58-67.

Follow these additional techniques and suggested embellishments unique to this Flower.

Satin Stitch Center

1. Trace ⅜" circle on template plastic, and cut out.
   You can substitute template with small button.

2. Draw ⅜" circle in center of Flower.

3. Bring needle threaded with two strand of yellow
   floss up at one edge of circle, and insert at opposite
   edge. Sew through fabric only.

4. Return to starting line by carrying floss underneath
   fabric. Make stitches close together to cover circle
   completely.

5. French Knots can also be stitched in center.

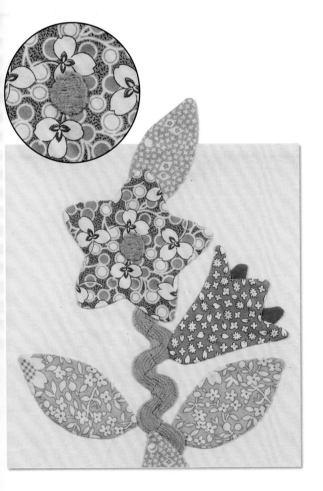

*Fussy cut Flower with shading on outside edge to give the
appearance of roundness.*

Zinnia

Zinnia A Lovely Addition To Magic Vine Quilt

When Nancy brought out the eighteenth block she said, "I think that you are all experienced enough now to be able to make difficult Flowers. The one I have for you today looks rather complicated, and I don't know but that it is. You will find there are a number of pieces but if you will follow the pattern carefully there ought to be no trouble.

Cut ten petals like the large ones and four small ones like the petals which partially show and which are drawn with the squared lines.

While the members were following all these directions they discussed the colors they were using for the Zinnia. Some members chose soft tans and orange for the small pieces of petals which showed in four different places.

Others chose pink and soft red. And some chose lavender and dull purple. It all depended upon the color they liked or the scraps of material they had on hand. In every case they were careful to choose fast color material, either plain or figured.

The overlapping leaf which partially covers the seam joining two blocks together was cut from the darker green gingham and the two whole leaves and stem were cut from the lighter green.

This scheme was used all through the second and fourth vines, while the first and third reversed the process.

Since the fourth block is a duplicate of the second it was necessary to make two Zinnia blocks.

The centers were worked with large French knots in a fast color embroidery cotton. The color may be yellow or the darker of the two shades used in the petals.

Copyright, 1930

1. Optional: Photocopy page and place on light table.

2. Place 7½" Background square on Placement Page.

3. Trace Stem line.

4. Cut 4½" long bias Stem and sew to Background square with your chosen method.

Yardage and Patterns

Cut one set for each block.

 Petals
Dark Yellow
5" x 5"

 Base
Yellow
6" x 5"

 Center
Button
Yellow Embroidery Floss

 Leaves and Stem
Green
3½" x 4"
4½" bias

 Overlapping Leaf
Green
2" x 3"

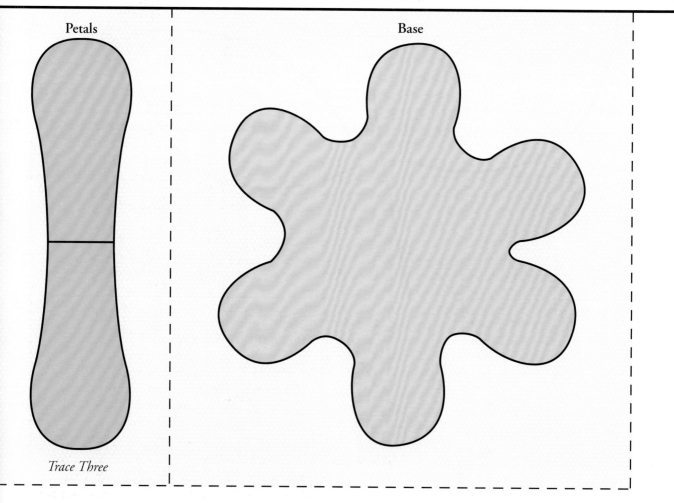

Petals

Base

Trace Three

134

Quick Turn Flowers: Follow general directions on pages 36-57.
Raw Edge Flowers: Follow general directions on pages 58-67.

Follow these additional techniques and suggested embellishments unique to this Flower.

Quick Turn Zinnia

1. Sew Stem, three Leaves, and base. Do not stuff base. Fuse in place.

2. Make three sets of Petals. Cut in half. Do not stuff.

3. Thread hand sewing needle with double strand of matching thread, and knot.

4. Run a long gathering stitch along raw edges of Petals. Pull thread tight and knot, connecting six Petals. Do not clip thread.

5. Push needle through center to attach Petals, and knot on back. Clip thread.

6. Fuse Petals, and sew around outside edges.

7. In center, sew on button, or French Knots, or Beads.

Silver trim petals on Raw Edge Flower to make a bit more slender. Fuse Base layer first and sew around outside edges. Fuse and sew petals one at a time. Trace around spool of thread or button for circle, fuse, and sew.

Pansy

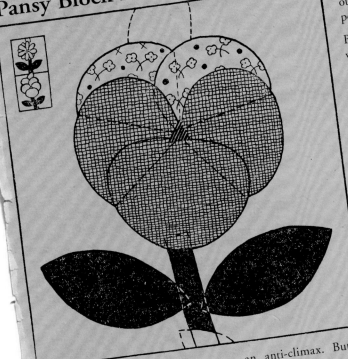

Pansy Block Follows Zinnia in Magic Vine Quilt

upper ones in one. Then I can outline the places where one petal overlaps another."

But the majority said they would rather cut five pieces, appliqueing the petals separately and overlapping them as shown by the dotted lines in the pattern.

In this block, as in the Zinnia, the members chose their own colors for the Flower. Some made tawny yellow pansies, others used the lavender and purple shades. Some of these were figured prints and others were plain, but in every case she was sure the colors were fast.

The members had a wonderful time recalling references to the pansy in literature, poetry and plays. One member insisted it belong to Johnny Jump-up family, and another called it Heart's Ease. They finished the discussion just as they finished the second Pansy Block and put the slanting stitches in the heart of the Flower. These stitches were done in heavy outline stitch, using a fast color embroidery cotton.

Copyright, 1930

The Nancy Page Quilt Club members were so enthusiastic about the last block they had made, the Zinnia, that Nancy feared the Pansy block would seem an anti-climax. But it proved fully as popular as the preceding patterns. Margaret, who wasn't overly ambitious, liked it because it had fewer pieces than the Zinnia.

She said when she looked at the pattern that she could cut the Flower from two pieces of cloth. "I can make the three lower petals in one piece and the two

1. Optional: Photocopy page and place on light table.

2. Place 7½" Background square on Placement Page.

3. Trace Stem line.

4. Cut 4" long bias Stem and sew to Background square with your chosen method.

Yardage and Patterns

Cut one set for each block.

 Back Petal
Red
2½" x 4½"

 Middle Petals
Red
2½" x 4¼"

 Front Petal
Red
2¼" x 3"

 Center
Fussy Cut 1½" square
Yellow Embroidery Floss

 Leaves and Stem
Green
3½" x 4"
4" bias

 Overlapping Leaf
Green
2" x 3"

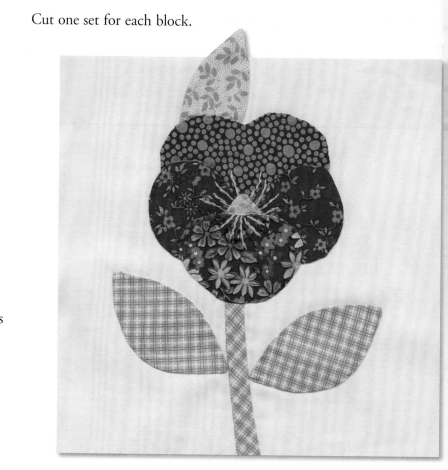

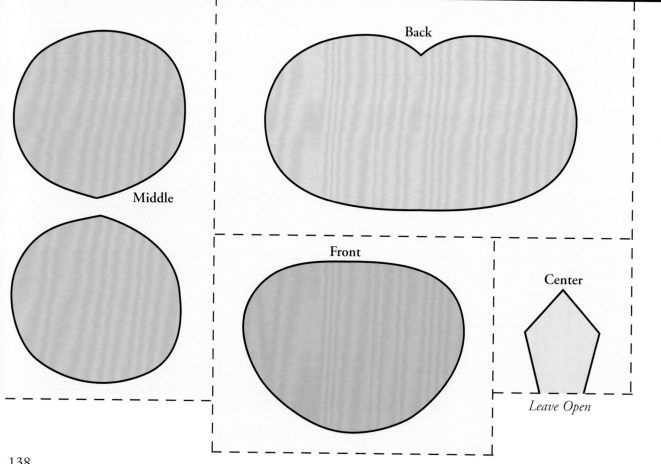

Middle

Back

Front

Center

Leave Open

Quick Turn Flowers: Follow general directions on pages 36-57.
Raw Edge Flowers: Follow general directions on pages 58-67.

Follow these additional techniques and suggested embellishments unique to this Flower.

Quick Turn Pansy

1. Place four petals on Background, leaving triangular open space in shape of a triangle.

2. Fussy Cut shaded fabric for Center.

3. Sew slanting stitches in center with yellow embroidery floss.

Folded Center

1. In place of a Fussy Cut, make a folded center from a 1½" square.

2. Fold square on diagonal.

3. Fold ends in.

4. Insert in open space.

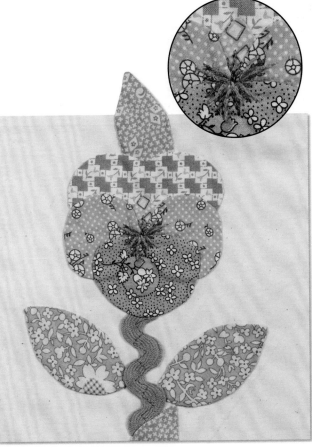

Tiger Lily

"All right, teacher, we'll try. But it looks rather difficult."

Nancy suggested that the Tiger Lily be developed in a yellow figured print with a small petal of rather brilliant orange. She said that the three upper petals, which are cut all in one piece, by the way, should be appliqued with the wrong side of the material outside and the lower two with the right side out.

One member wanted to use a pink and white material, to make that pink and white field lily. But most of the group chose the real Tiger Lily shades.

The stamens are worked in outline and satin stitch, using fast color embroidery cotton in yellow.

Don't forget that this block appears in the fourth vine as well as in the second, so two Tiger Lily blocks must be made.

Tiger Lily adds challenge to MagicVine

You should have heard the Nancy Page Club members groan when they saw the Tiger Lily block. "Oh, Nancy, have a heart. That Flower is too hard. Look at those curves on the petals. We never can make those."

1. Optional: Photocopy page and place on light table.

2. Place 7½" Background square on Placement Page.

3. Trace Stem line.

4. Cut 4" long bias Stem and sew to Background square with your chosen method.

Yardage and Patterns

Cut one set for each block.

Upper Petals
Dark Orange
3¾" x 6¼"

Lower Petals
Light Orange
2" x 6"

Bottom
Green
1½" x 2"

Stamens
Black and Brown
Embroidery Floss

Leaves and Stem
Green
3½" x 4"
4" bias

Overlapping Leaf
Green
2" x 3"

Leave Open

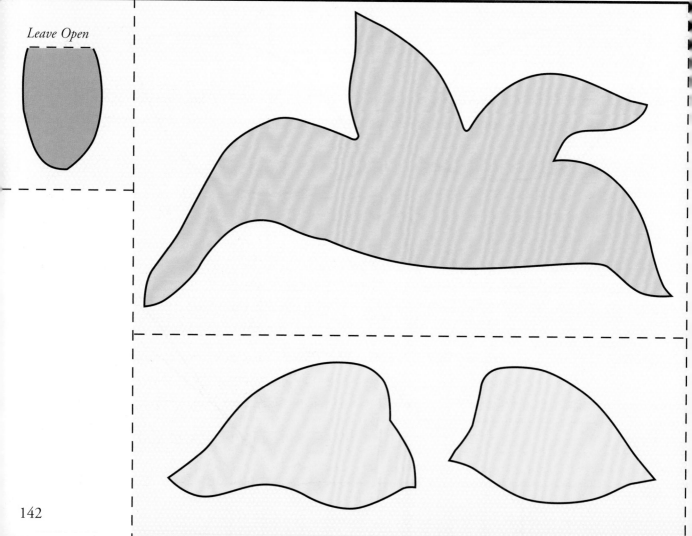

Quick Turn Flowers: Follow general directions on pages 36-57.

Raw Edge Flowers: Follow general directions on pages 58-67.

Follow these additional techniques and suggested embellishments unique to this Flower.

Placing Petals

1. Fuse green bottom #1 on Stem first. Sew around outside edge.

2. Fuse Overlapping Leaf #2 for Straight Set block and dark orange upper #3 Petals next.

3. Fuse lower Petals #4 last.

Raw Edge Flower

1. Photocopy with mirror image feature on copier so flowers are placed the same as on Placement Page.

2. If you don't have a photocopier, turn pattern page over so printing is on bottom, and trace.

3. Do not mirror image Placement Page.

Stitching Center

1. Hand sew stem stitch lines and make French Knots on the ends.

2. Machine sew lines with lightning stitch and sew black beads on ends.

Sew a back stitch with #5 gold pearl cotton and finish with beads.

Patterns were mirror imaged when photocopied so the finished Raw Edge Flower looks like the Quick Turn Flower.

Forget Me Not

Forget-Me-Not Enhances Charming Magic Vine

"My, I'm glad you have put in the Forget-Me-Not, Nancy." This was the general comment from the members of the Nancy Page Quilt Club when they saw the twenty-first block in the series. But by this time the club members were so experienced that they never batted an eyelash when they saw the pattern.

Nancy counted on their enthusiasm for the little Flower to carry them past any difficulties in the making. And at that, there weren't so many.

The Forget-Me-Not appears in both the second and the fourth long vine on the quilt, so two blocks have to be made.

The members chose light blue fast color cloth for the Flowers.

One Flower was cut from pale blue, another from a darker blue.

All the Flowers as given in the pattern are the same, so that one paper pattern will do for the four Flowers.

The centers of the Flowers are done in white embroidery cotton with radiating stitches in lazy daisy stitch in soft yellow.

The two leaves extending from the stem and the stem itself were cut from green gingham of the light shade. The leaf which connects the Tiger Lily block with the Forget-Me-Not block is cut from green of a darker shade.

Copyright, 1930

Placement Page

1. Optional: Photocopy page and place on light table.

2. Place 7½" Background square on Placement Page.

3. Trace Stem line.

4. Cut 6½" long bias Stem and sew to Background square with your chosen method.

Yardage and Patterns

 One Flower
First Blue
2½" x 3"

 Three Flowers
Second Blue
2½" x 7¼"

 Four Centers
¼" Yellow Buttons
or White and Yellow
Embroidery Floss

 Leaves and Stem
Green
3½" x 4"
6½" bias

 Overlapping Leaf
Green
2" x 3"

Cut one set for each block.

Quick Turn Flowers: Follow general directions on pages 36-57.
Raw Edge Flowers: Follow general directions on pages 58-67.

Follow these additional techniques and suggested embellishments unique to this Flower.

Dimensional Forget Me Not

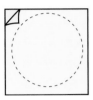   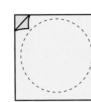

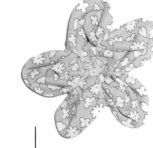

1. Cut (6) 3½" squares from one blue, and (2) 3½" squares from second blue.

2. Place two matching squares right sides together. Make four pairs.

3. Make 2¾" circle template. Trace 2¾" circle on each, sew on the line and trim ⅛" from line.

4. Cut a small hole in the center, and turn right side out.

5. Place fabric circle on pattern sheet, and mark each circle into five equal parts.

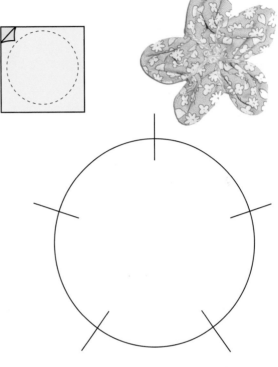

6. Thread an embroidery needle with an 18" strand of yellow pearl cotton and knot on the backside. From the back, bring the thread up in the center, wrap it around one mark, and bring thread up in the center again. Pull slightly. Continue wrapping pearl cotton on marks and pulling slightly.

7. Sew three French Knots in the center.

Nasturtium

Yellow Print Nasturtium Enlivens Magic Vine

that, not that there is a white space left between the three upper petals. This is the first time that the pattern has been drawn in this fashion. Since it is rather difficult it will be a wise person who follows directions exactly.

Choose the fast color materials which you use for the Nasturtiums. These had best be prints in yellows and soft browns. The calyx on each Flower may be of green or of pale yellow.

The leaves and stem are cut from the light green material and the overlapping leaf indicated by the dotted line at the top of the pattern is cut from darker green gingham. This leaf uses the pattern given in block number two.

Work the center of the Flower with fast color deep orange embroidery cotton.

The members counted the Flowers and realized that the next one would be the last. They guessed and guessed as to what the Flower would be. Nancy told them it was yellow. That gave them a clue. Does it do the same for you?

Copyright, 1930

The club members were unanimous in declaring that the last blocks in the second and fourth vines were the prettiest of all. "I loved the Forget-Me-Not when I had it finished," this from Bertha, a rather shy and quiet member. "My husband said the Zinnia was the prettiest one I had made," this from Jane.

"Well, I have liked the others, but here is my favorite," and Peggy pointed to the pattern for the day – the Nasturtium. "It may be your favorite, Peg, but look at those curves. I wager you don't think so highly of it when you are working with it." Of course you know it was Margaret who said this. But the pattern is rather tricky, at

1. Optional: Photocopy page and place on light table.

2. Place 7½" Background square on Placement Page.

3. Trace Stem line.

4. Cut 4¼" long bias Stem and sew to Background square with your chosen method.

Yardage and Patterns

 Top Petals and Bud
Orange
4" x 5½"

 Bottom Petals
Yellow
1½" x 4"

 Center
Beads and
Embroidery Floss

 Accent Bases
Green
2" x 2½"

 Leaves and Stem
Green
3½" x 4"
4¼" bias

 Overlapping Leaf
Green
2" x 3"

Cut one set for each block.

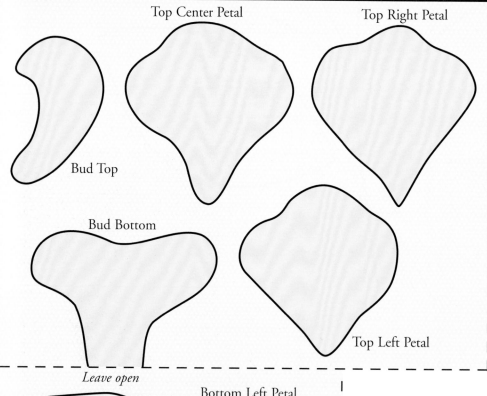

Top Center Petal

Top Right Petal

Bud Base

Bud Top

Bud Bottom

Top Left Petal

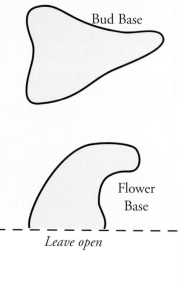

Flower Base

Leave open

Leave open

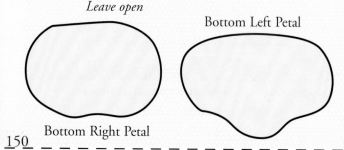

Bottom Left Petal

Bottom Right Petal

Quick Turn Flowers: Follow general directions on pages 36-57.
Raw Edge Flowers: Follow general directions on pages 58-67.

Follow these additional techniques and suggested embellishments unique to this Flower.

Quick Turn Flower

1. Turn pieces with small straw and ball point bodkin or 2.35mm crochet hook and small straw.

2. Fuse petals in order beginning with Flower Base.

Raw Edge Flower

1. The best approach to this Flower is to mirror image all pattern pieces on a photo copier. When patterns are mirror imaged, patterns fit properly on the Placement Page.

2. In this example, patterns were not mirror imaged. To make Flowers fit, the Stem was curved to the right, and the two Flowers were reversed.

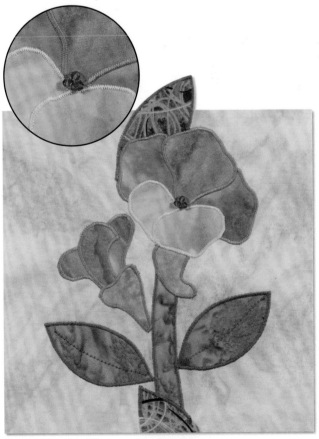

Knot after each bead on back side so only one bead will fall off if it gets loose, instead of all of them.

For Raw Edge Flower only, mirror image pattern.

Buttercup

Plaid Buttercup Last Blossom on Magic Vine

The last Flower for the Magic Vine Quilt was yellow as Nancy had said – it was the Buttercup.

They used a gay, fast color plaid in yellow for the opened Flower and some of that as well as a plain yellow for the two partially opened ones. The French knots were done in yellow fast color embroidery cotton.

The leaf which covers part of the joining of the Nasturtium block to the white square which will hold the Buttercup was cut from dark green gingham and appliqued before the Buttercups were put on.

The stem and leaves were cut from green gingham of a lighter shade. They were appliqued in place. A duplicate of this block was made for the last Flower in the fourth vine and then the four long vines were finished.

It was with a feeling of sadness that the members gathered at Nancy's house for the last meeting of the quilt club. True, they still had the border to finish and the binding to put on and the quilting to do, but this was the beginning of the end.

Copyright, 1930

1. Optional: Photocopy page and place on light table.

2. Place 7½" Background square on Placement Page.

3. Trace Stem line.

4. Cut 5½" long bias Stem and sew to Background square with your chosen method.

If you are making vines exactly as the Nancy Page Club members, this is the last block in the second and fourth rows for Full/Queen and King, and does not have an Overlapping Leaf at the bottom of the Stem.

Yardage and Patterns

 Top Petals
Yellow
3" x 5½"

 Underneath Petals
Dark Yellow
1½" x 4"

 Joining Stem
Green
1" x 2"

 Center
Brown Embroidery Floss

 Leaves and Stems
Green
3½" x 4"
5½" bias

 Overlapping Leaf
Green
1½" x 3"

Cut one set for each block.

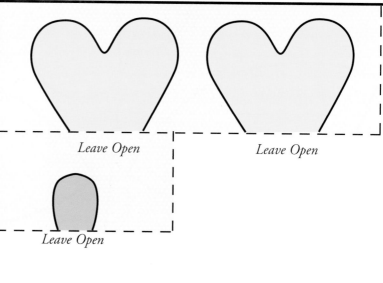

Leave Open

Leave Open

Leave Open

Quick Turn Flowers: Follow general directions on pages 36-57.

Raw Edge Flowers: Follow general directions on pages 58-67.

Follow these additional techniques and suggested embellishments unique to this Flower.

Placing Petals

1. Place joining Stem touching main Stem.

2. Place underneath petals next.

3. Place top petals last.

4. Embellish with French Knots or glass beads.

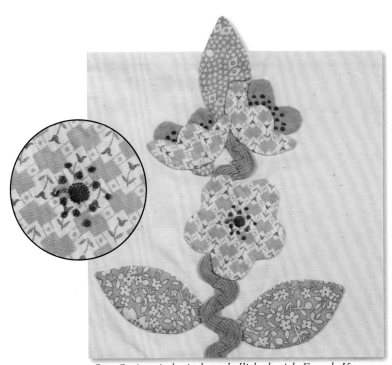

Sew Satin stitch circle embellished with French Knots.

Mottled fabric, a stripe, plus a small print combined together make a charming country block.

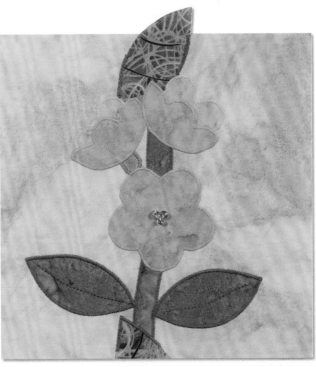

Make Stem in two parts so green doesn't show under yellow.

Quilts with Blocks
Set Straight in Vertical Rows

Elisabeth graced her Vine Border with wild roses and finished with a Rainbow Binding. She achieved a fashionable appeal to her quilt by using contemporary fabrics for her Flowers and setting her blocks in three straight rows.

Pieced and Quilted by Elisabeth Pfeiffer 51" x 63"

Teresa arranged her blocks in three straight rows and used jumbo green rickrack for her Stems and Border with random Leaves and wild roses. She opted for a Rainbow Binding to reflect her 1930's reproduction fabric flowers.

Pieced by Teresa Varnes
Quilted by Carol Selepec
58" x 70"

157

Sewing Blocks in Straight Vertical Rows

If you are creating your own order of Flowers, plan placement of blocks with equal spacing of colors and shapes, and Vines weaving back and forth.

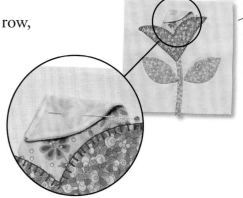

1. Lay out Flower blocks in order. The top block in each row does not have an Overlapping Leaf.

2. Fold back Overlapping Leaf on second block in first row, and pin.

3. Flip second block right sides together to first block.

4. Sew with ¼" seam. Press seam toward second block.

5. Press top of Overlapping Leaf to bottom of first block, covering bottom edge of Stem.

6. Finish outside edge of Overlapping Leaf with your chosen method.

7. Continue sewing blocks and Overlapping Leaves into rows.

8. The last block in each row does not have a Leaf at the bottom of the Stem.

Sewing Rows Together

1. Lay out vertical rows of Flowers. Make sure all rows are the same length.

2. Measure length of rows, and cut Lattice strips the same size. If necessary, piece strips together to get length.

3. Place Lattice on left side of Flower rows. Flip right sides together with Flowers on top.

4. Line up top and bottom of Lattice with Flowers and pin together in several places. Sew Flowers to Lattice.

5. Press seams toward Lattice.

6. Pin and sew vertical rows together, lining up blocks straight across.

7. Sew Lattice to right side of last row.

8. Press seams toward Lattice.

9. Sew Lattice to top and bottom, trim and press seams toward Lattice.

Wallhanging - 2 Rows of Flowers

Magic Vine

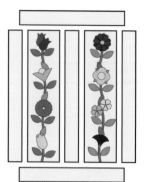

*Wallhanging -
2 Rows of 4 Flowers*

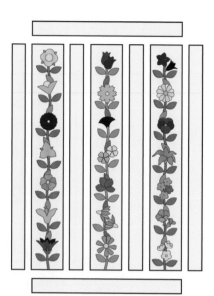

Lap - 3 Rows of 7 Flowers each

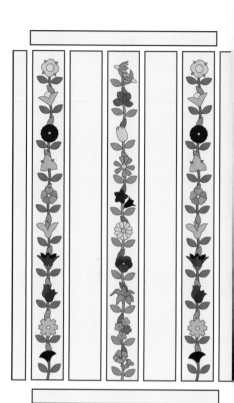

Twin - 3 Rows of 10 Flowers each

*The stunning brown background provides
the perfect backdrop for Sue's pink toned
Flowers. Her Folded Border and Scalloped
Edge grace her quilt for a lovely finish.*

*Pieced by Sue Bouchard
Quilted by Amie Potter
32" x 43"*

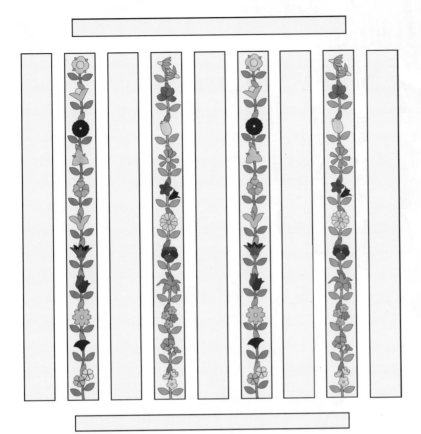

Full/Queen - 4 Rows of 11 Flowers each

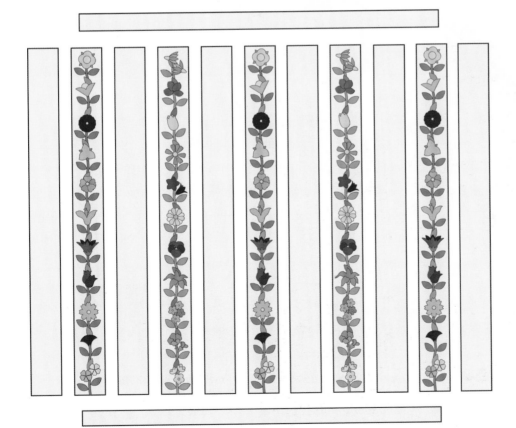

King - 5 Rows of 11 Flowers each

Quilts with Blocks
On Point with Solid Squares

With yellow checks for Solid Squares and Outside Border, Eleanor's quilt brings to mind a summer day. The jumbo rickrack Stems and Inside Border add just the right touch of whimsy. She finished with a Wave Edge and picked a posy for the lower right hand corner.

Pieced by Eleanor Burns
Quilted by Amie Potter
40" x 50"

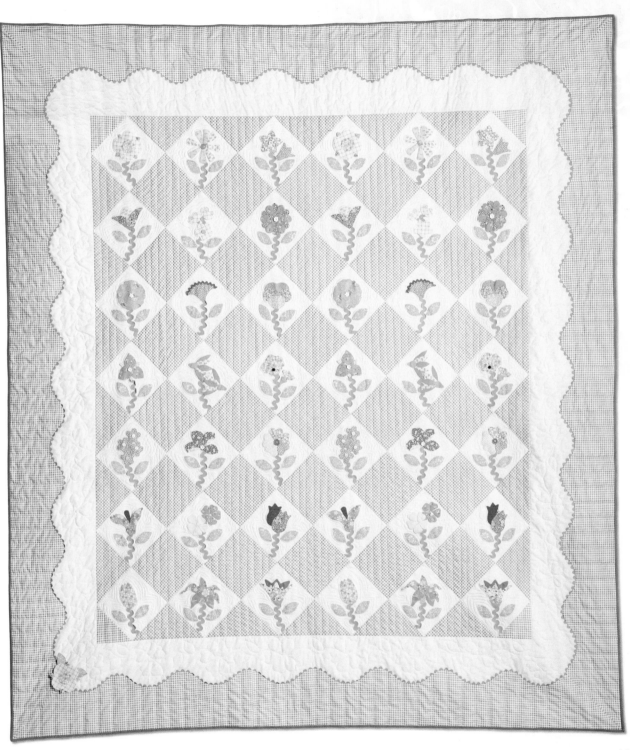

Marcia's cheerful Flowers are balanced on jumbo rickrack Stems.
From the directions in Fans & Flutterbys by Patricia Knoechel,
Marcia created a Scalloped Inner Border, trimmed with blue
rickrack and finished her quilt with a straight edge.

Pieced by Marcia Woolf
Quilted by Cindee Ferris
83" x 92"

163

Sewing Blocks On Point with Solid Squares

1. Cut setting fabric into Solid Squares and Side and Corner Triangles. For Solid Squares, cut 7½" selvage to selvage strips into 7½" squares.

	Number of 7½" strips	Number of 7½" squares
Wallhanging	1 strip	4 squares
Lap	2 strips	6 squares
Twin	4 strips	18 squares
Full/Queen	6 strips	30 squares
King	8 strips	36 squares

2. Cut fabric for Side and Corner Triangles into 13" selvage to selvage strips, then into 6½" squares and 11½" squares.

	Number of 13" strips	Number of 6½" squares	Number of 11½" squares
Wallhanging	1 strip	2 squares	2 squares
Lap	1 strip	2 squares	3 squares
Twin	2 strips	2 squares	5 squares
Full/Queen	2 strips	2 squares	6 squares
King	2 strips	2 squares	6 squares

3. From 13" strip, cut two 6½" squares first, and then 11½" squares, or as many as needed.

6½"	11½"	11½"	11½"
6½"			

4. Lay out Flower blocks with Solid Squares. See layouts on pages 166-167.

5. Sew blocks together in diagonal rows.

6. Press seams toward Solid Squares.

7. Cut 11½" squares for Side Triangles on both diagonals.

Cut into fourths.

8. Place Side Triangles on ends of rows.

9. Sew on Side Triangles. Press seams toward Triangles. Trim tips even with blocks.

10. Sew diagonal rows together.

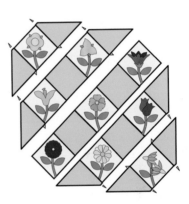

11. Cut two 6½" Corner squares in half on one diagonal.

Cut in half.

12. Sew on Corner Triangles. Press seams toward Triangles.

13. Straighten outside edges. Allow ¼" seam on all sides.

14. Sew optional rickrack to top. Rickrack is on page 166.

15. Add First Border. Turn to **Borders and Border Treatments** on page 181.

Wallhanging - 9 Blocks

Lap - 12 Blocks

Twin - 28 Blocks

Sewing Optional Rickrack Around Outside Edge of Top

1. Line up edge of rickrack with edge of top.

2. Place open toe foot on sewing machine.

3. Sew down center of rickrack with straight basting stitch.

4. Sew next Border with seam wider than rickrack seam to cover basting stitches.

Yardage for Rickrack	Outside Edge
Wallhanging	2½ yds
Lap	4 yds
Twin	6 yds
Full/Queen	7½ yds
King	8 yds

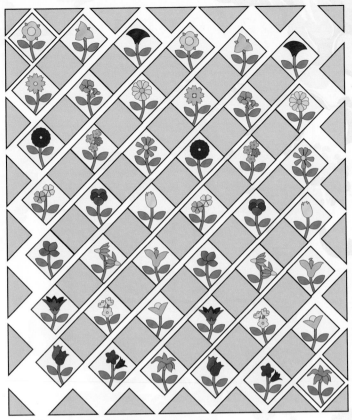

Full/Queen - 42 Blocks

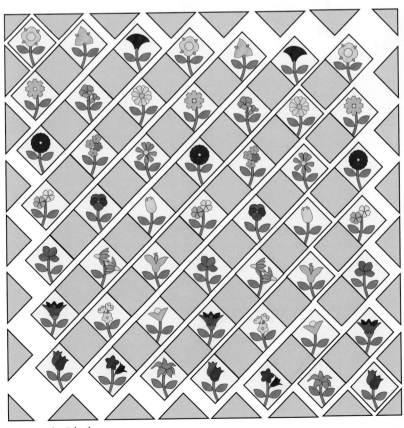

King - 49 Blocks

Quilts with Blocks On Point with Lattice

Patricia first chose a 3½" border print for her Lattice and selected her colors for six Flowers to match. Her Scalloped Edge with Bias Binding creates the perfect finish.

Pieced by Patricia Knoechel
Quilted by Amie Potter
55" x 66"

Teresa started with a border print of 5½" and 3½" stripes to direct her color choices for her Flowers. Her Straight Edge finish with a complimentary green Binding keeps the quilt balanced for this perky lap quilt.

Pieced by Teresa Varnes
Quilted by Janna Mitchell
45" x 58"

169

Sewing Blocks On Point with Lattice

1. Cut Side and Corner Triangle fabric into 13" selvage to selvage strips.

2. From 13" strip, cut two 6½" squares first, and three 11½" squares, or as many as needed.

Number of	13" Strips	6½" Squares	11½" Squares
Wallhanging	1 strip	4 squares	2 squares
Lap	3 strips	6 squares	6 squares
Twin	3 strips	6 squares	9 squares
Full/Queen	5 strips	10 squares	15 squares
King	6 strips	12 squares	18 squares

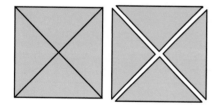

3. Cut 11½" squares for Side Triangles on both diagonals.

4. Lay out Flower blocks in vertical rows with Side Triangles. See layouts on pages 176-177.

Number of Flowers and Rows

Wallhanging	6 Flowers, 2 Rows of three each
Lap	15 Flowers, 3 Rows of five each
Twin	21 Flowers, 3 Rows of seven each
Full/Queen	35 Flowers, 5 Rows of seven each
King	42 Flowers, 6 Rows of seven each

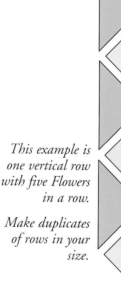

This example is one vertical row with five Flowers in a row.

Make duplicates of rows in your size.

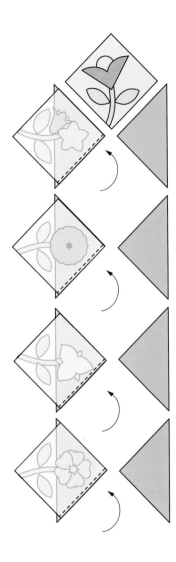

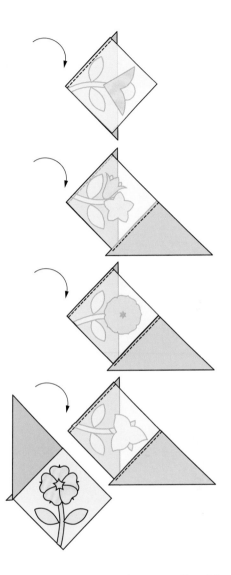

5. Starting with second block from top, flip blocks up to the left. Match square corners and pin with tip extending. Stack paired blocks, and assembly-line sew with triangle on bottom to prevent bias from stretching.

6. Clip blocks apart, and press seams toward triangles. Return to layout.

7. Starting at the top, flip blocks down to the right. Leave last block in layout. Match up square corners and pin. Stack paired blocks from bottom up, and assembly-line sew, starting from the square corners.

8. Clip blocks apart, and press seams toward triangles.

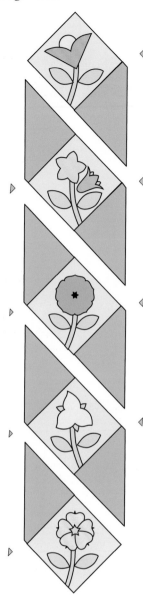

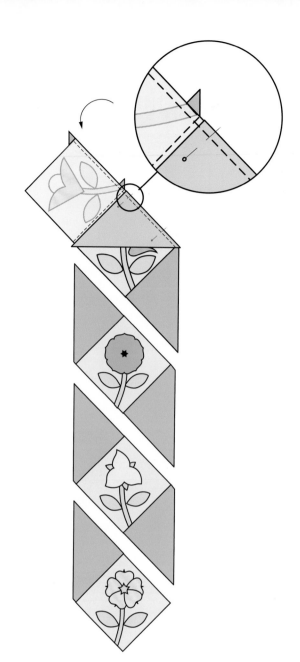

9. Trim tips even with blocks.

10. Return to layout.

11. Flip top row down to second row. Match center seam, pin and sew.

12. Continue sewing rows together.

13. Press diagonal seams down toward bottom of quilt. Trim tips even with blocks.

Adding Corner Triangles

1. Cut 6½" Corner squares in half on one diagonal.

Number of Squares

Wallhanging	4
Lap	6
Twin	6
Full/Queen	10
King	12

2. Fold triangles in half and press. Open.

3. Fold top and bottom blocks on two opposite corners in half, press and open. Pin center of triangle to center of block on two opposite corners. Let tips hang over on ends. Pin.

4. Sew with triangles on bottom.

5. Set seams with triangle on top, open and press seams toward triangle. Trim tips.

6. Repeat with remaining two corners.

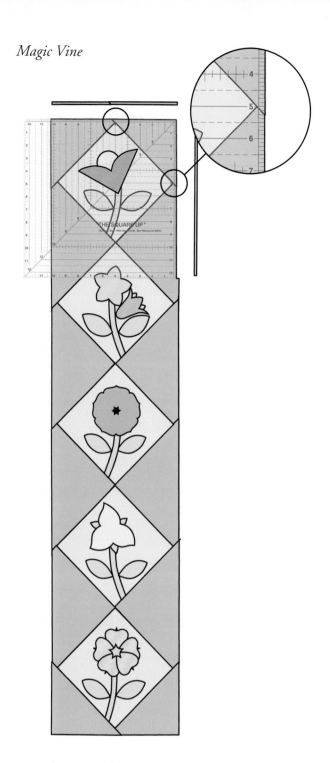

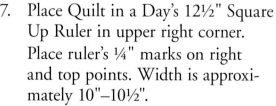

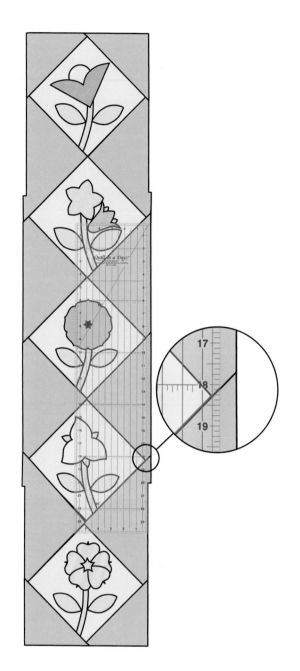

7. Place Quilt in a Day's 12½" Square Up Ruler in upper right corner. Place ruler's ¼" marks on right and top points. Width is approximately 10"–10½".

8. Trim right and top corners, leaving ¼" seam allowance.

9. Turn Square Up Ruler and trim left side, leaving ¼" seam allowance.

10. Trim opposite corners.

11. Line up 6" x 24" Ruler's diagonal line with seams, and trim ¼" from points where seams cross.

Sewing Vertical Rows with Lattice

1. Lay out vertical rows of Flowers.

2. Measure length of rows, and cut Lattice strips. If necessary, piece strips together to get length.

3. Place Lattice on left side of Flower row. Flip right sides together with Flowers on top, pin and sew.

4. Press seams toward Lattice.

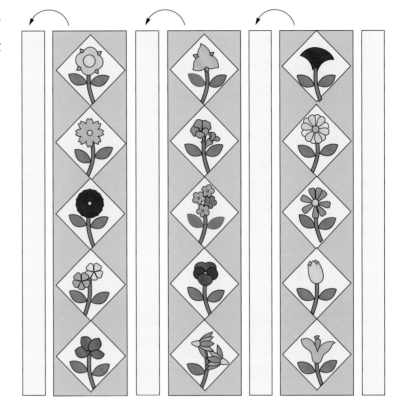

5. Pin and sew vertical rows together, lining up Flowers straight across.

6. Sew Lattice to right side of last row.

7. Press seams toward Lattice.

8. Sew Lattice to top and bottom, trim, and press seams toward Lattice.

Magic Vine

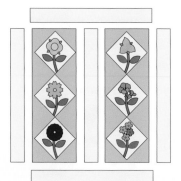

Wallhanging - 6 Blocks

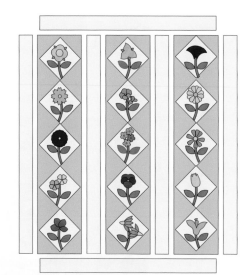

Lap - 15 Blocks

Twin - 21 Blocks

Pieced by Teresa Varnes
Quilted by Amie Potter
36" x 42"

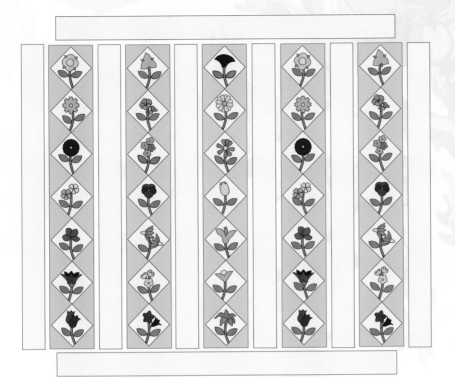

Full/Queen - 35 Blocks

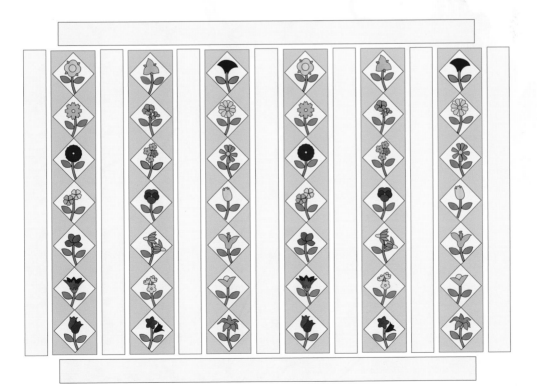

King - 42 Blocks

Borders and Border Treatment

There are four different ways to add color to your Borders.

Folded Border - page 180

Using neon batiks, Beverly created a contemporary wallhanging. She used an extra wide Folded Border to set off her Flower blocks and finished with a straight edge.

Pieced by Beverly Burris
Quilted by Carol Selepec
34" x 34"

Vine and Leaves Border - page 184

Patricia chose to use tone on tone white Background and Lattice to display her Flowery Vines. In her Leaf Border, she arranged the Leaves to flow in coordinated directions.

Pieced by Patricia Knoechel
Quilted by Amie Potter
72" x 98"

Rainbow Border - page 182

A mottled green fabric provides a soft palette for Bette's flowering Vines. She mirrored her Flower colors in her Rainbow Border, scalloped her edges and finished off with medium green Binding.

Pieced by Bette Rhodaback
Quilted by Sandy Lachowski
48" x 68

Stripe with Miter - page 190

Teresa allowed her choice of the 5½" border with Mitered Corners to direct the colors of her Flowers in this lovely wallhanging. Her 3½" center Lattice is the companion stripe to her Outside Border. Green checkered fabric to match her Leaves provides the perfect Binding.

Pieced by Teresa Varnes
Quilted by Janna Mitchell
33" x 39"

Adding Optional Folded Border

The Folded Border can be added before or after First Border.

1. If sides of quilt are longer than 1¼" Folded Border strips, piece Folded Border strips together. Press seams open.

2. Press 1¼" strips in half lengthwise, wrong sides together.

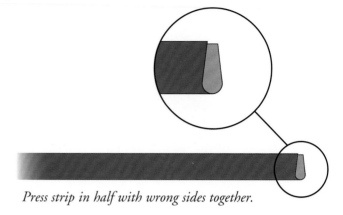

Press strip in half with wrong sides together.

3. Place Folded Border on two opposite sides, matching raw edges.

4. Sew ⅛" seam from raw edges with 10 stitches per inch or 3.0 on a computerized machine. Trim even with sides of quilt top. **Do not fold out.**

5. Repeat on remaining two sides, overlapping at corners.

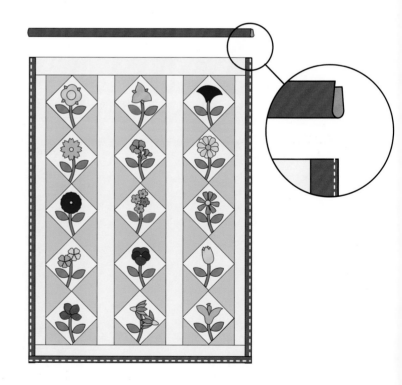

Adding Borders

1. Cut Border strips according to your Yardage Chart.

2. Trim selvages.

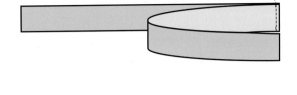

3. Lay first strip right side up. Lay second strip right sides to it. Backstitch, stitch and backstitch again.

4. Continue assembly-line sewing all short ends together into long pieces.

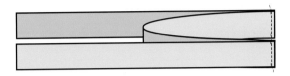

5. Measure length of both sides and length through center of quilt top.

6. Cut two Border strips the average length.

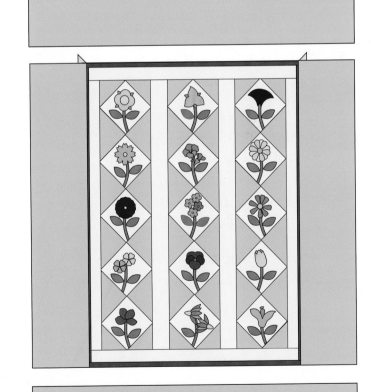

7. Place Border right sides together to sides of pieced top. Pin layers together in center, on ends, and several places between.

8. Sew to sides.

9. Set seam with Border on top. Open and press seams toward Border.

10. Measure width in several places. Cut two Border pieces for top and bottom the average width. Pin and sew.

11. Press seams toward Border.

12. Sew optional Folded Border, rickrack or Rainbow Border.

13. Continue adding remaining Borders.

Making Optional Rainbow Border

1. Plan where to place Rainbow Border. Measure length and width. Divide each measurement by 7½" to figure out how many 2" x 8" pieces are needed.

2. Arrange colors beside top.

Arrange colors beside top.

3. Assembly-line sew two sets of 2" x 8" pieces approximately 5" longer than length.

4. Assembly-line sew two sets approximately 8" longer than width.

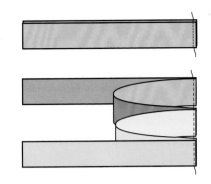

5. Center lengthwise Rainbow Borders on sides, pin, sew and trim excess on both ends.

6. Press seams toward Lattice.

7. Center widthwise Rainbow Borders on top and bottom, pin, sew and trim excess. Press seams toward Lattice.

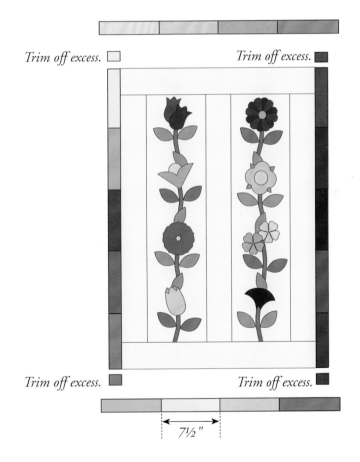

Trim off excess.   *Trim off excess.*

Trim off excess.   *Trim off excess.*

7½ "

Quilts with Vine and Leaves Border

The border of Vines and Leaves provide a lovely frame for Eleanor's magic garden. She chose bright pastels for her Flowers in three straight rows. Her light green Background and Binding give her quilt a spring-time quality.

Pieced by Eleanor Burns
Quilted by Amie Potter
46" x 66"

Sewing Optional Vine and Leaves to Border

Determining Number and Size of Vines

Vines can be stitched to last Border before or after it is sewn to quilt top.

1. Draw lines on corners of outside Border using a hera marker or chalk marker so marks can be removed. Blue lines on the illustrations represent chalk lines.

2. Mark centers of Vine Border strips as guidelines.

3. Measure length and width excluding corners, and record measurements.

4. Decide how many curves per Vine to make on each side and top and bottom. Select odd numbers as 3, 5, 7, 9 or 11.

5. Divide length and width by odd numbers for size of curves.

6. Select the same size curves closest in measurement for both length and width.

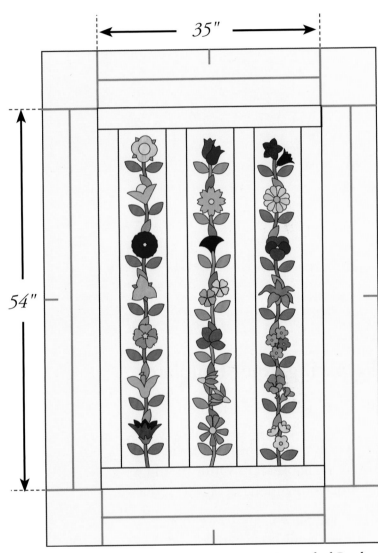

Unattached Borders:
Mark outside Border strips down the center. Place strips next to top, lining up centers of both.

Attached Borders:
Mark lengthwise guidelines in centers of Border with chalk or hera marker.

Example Width 35" x Length 54"

• Recalling multiplication tables will help you.
• Both of these numbers are divisible by 5 or 9. Think of 35 as 5 x 7 = 35 and 9 x 6 = 54.
• 35" ÷ 5 is 7. *Make five 7" curves on top and bottom.*
• 54" ÷ 9 is 6. *Make nine 6" curves on sides.*
The odd number is the number of curves.
The length divided by number of curves = size of curve.

7. As a quick check, mark off selected measurements with chalk and a regular ruler.

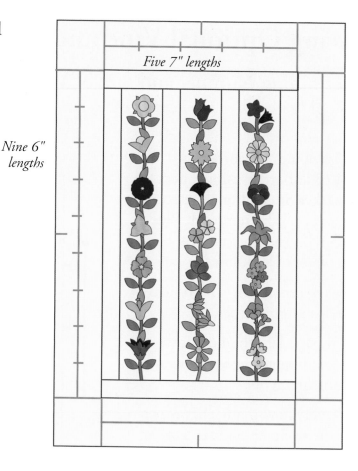

Five 7" lengths

Nine 6" lengths

Preparing Your Template

1. Find template pattern on page 229 in back of book and photocopy. A heavy acrylic ruler is available from Quilt in a Day for your purchase.

2. Glue photocopy to template plastic with glue stick, and cut out.

3. The top edge is for marking Vines in lengths of 4" to 9".

4. Place Glow-Line™ tape on template's selected measurement. As an extra check, measure the distance between the two marks with a regular ruler.

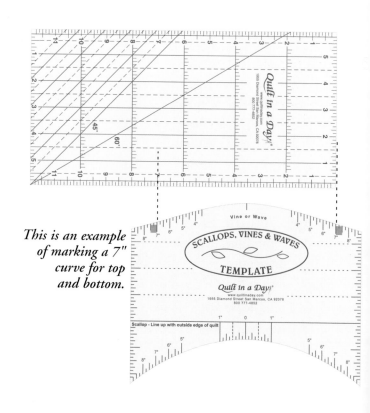

This is an example of marking a 7" curve for top and bottom.

Marking Vines

1. Start by placing vine template on corner line with shape of curve out toward edge of quilt. Line up selected size of curve on guide line.

2. Trace length of curve with disappearing pen or chalk. Put marks on ends.

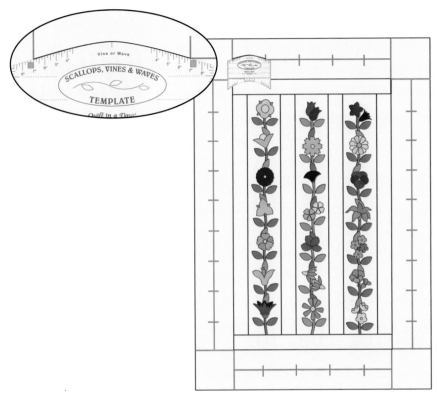

Top and Bottom are 7" curves.

3. Turn template around with shape of curve going in toward center of quilt. Place measurement on guide line, and match with marks. Trace curve for Vine.

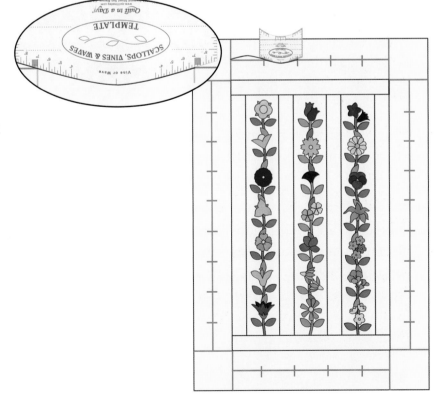

4. Continue marking curves from corners to center, alternating the direction of the Vine. You may need to elongate or shorten center.

5. Draw Vines on sides. Begin at corner placing shape of Vine out toward edge of quilt.

6. Continue marking curves from corners to center, alternating the direction of the Vine.

7. Round out corners.

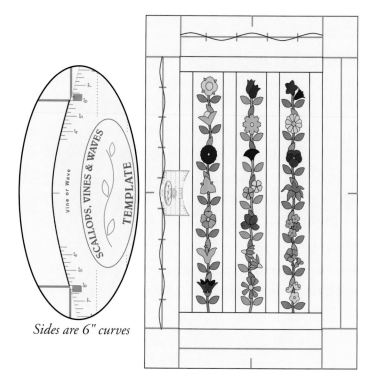

Sides are 6" curves

Cutting Bias for Vines and Strips for Leaves

1. Cut one 16" selvage to selvage strip for Wallhanging and Lap. Cut two 16" strips for Twin, Full/Queen and King.

2. Cut 16" strip into 1¼" bias strips.

Number of 1¼" bias strips for Vines

Wallhanging	10
Lap	13
Twin	19
Full/Queen	22
King	24

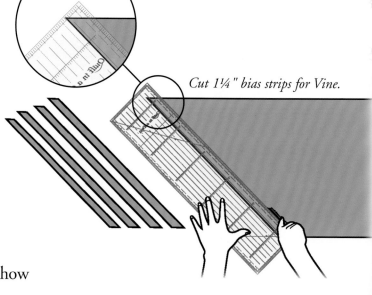

Cut 1¼ " bias strips for Vine.

3. Cut 3½" strips for Leaves. Follow directions for Quick Turn Leaves on pages 41-42 or Raw Edge Leaves on page 62.

4. These are approximations based on how many Leaves you choose to make.

Number of 3½" strips for Leaves

Wallhanging	2
Lap	3
Twin	3
Full/Queen	5
King	5

If you choose, make Stems out of one green fabric and Leaves out of a second green fabric.

5. Piece bias strips together lengthwise.

6. Press seams open. Press bias strips in half wrong sides together.

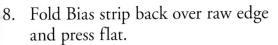

7. Starting on one end, place raw edges of Vine on curve of line. Sew scant ¼" seam.

   If Borders are not attached to each side, place raw edges of Vine toward outside edge of quilt so they will eventually match in corners.
   Leave 10" lengths on ends to sew together on corner once Borders are sewn to top.

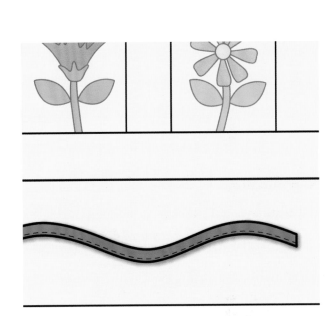

8. Fold Bias strip back over raw edge and press flat.

9. Sew folded edge to Background with your favorite method.

10. Make two Leaves for each curve, or as many as desired.

11. Sew Leaves to Vine by hand or machine. The easiest way to machine sew Leaves is by free motion with darning foot and feed dogs dropped.

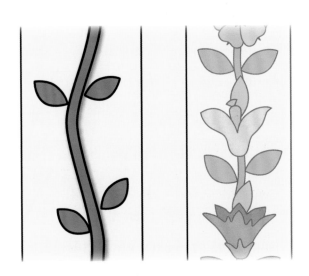

Optional Stripe Borders with Mitered Corners

Pieced by Teresa Varnes
Quilted by Janna Mitchell
45" x 58"

1. Calculate length of strip needed. The total length includes length of the quilt, plus two times the width of the stripe, plus 3" inches at each end to match the flower or design in the corner.

2. Cut the strip. Before cutting off end of stripe, lay out long side strips next to the quilt.

3. At a 45° angle, turn under one end of the stripe to see where the seam will fall. Ideally the seam will not fall on a large flower.

4. Adjust if necessary, and cut length of strips.

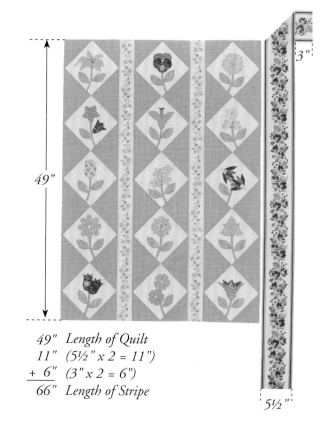

49"   *Length of Quilt*
11"   *(5½" x 2 = 11")*
+ 6"   *(3" x 2 = 6")*
66"   *Length of Stripe*

5. Flip a side stripe onto the quilt. On the wrong side of the stripe, mark a dot ¼" in from the top and bottom edges of the quilt. Continue making dots on remaining side border and pin.

6. Lockstitch on dot, and sew along the line printed on the fabric.

7. Stop sewing on the dot ¼" up from the bottom edge of the quilt, and lockstitch.

8. In same manner, sew stripe to opposite side of quilt.

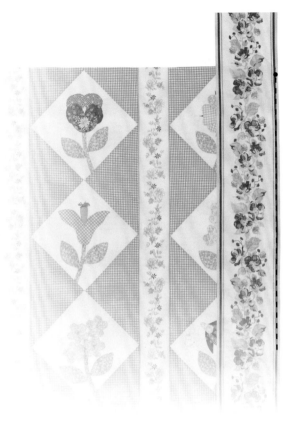

9. Sew top and bottom strips to quilt. Start and stop on dots. Seams will meet side strips ¼" in from edges.

Mitered Corner

1. Fold quilt diagonally to line up two stripes right sides together.

2. Line up the diagonal line on a 12½" Square Up ruler with the outside edge of the strips. Line up the right edge of the ruler with the dot where the stitches meet.

3. Draw a sewing line from the outside edge to the dot.

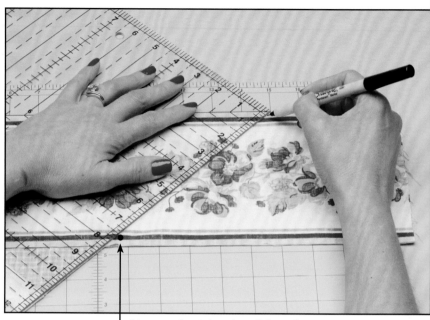

Line up the right edge of the ruler with the dot where the stitches meet.

4. Place pins at the points where the drawn line crosses the fabric line. Check pin alignment with the second stripe underneath.

5. Starting at the outside edge, stitch on the drawn line to the dot, and lockstitch.

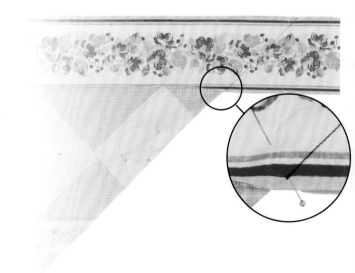

6. Trim seam allowance to ½" and press seams open.

7. Miter all four corners in this manner.

8. Press seams toward Border.

Optional Curved Outside Edges

Wave Outside Edge

These two outside edges are made easily with the help of the Scallop, Wave and Vine template provided on page 229. A heavy acrylic template is available from Quilt in a Day.

Gentle curves make up the Wave Edge. It's necessary to have an odd number of curves per side so corners match up. Since they are gentle, curves are easy to bind with bias strips. Waves add more interest to the edges, carrying through an old-fashioned theme.

Pieced by Eleanor Burns
Quilted by Amie Potter
40" x 50"

Scallop Outside Edge

On the Scallop Edge, it's not necessary to have an odd number of scallops per side. With narrow bias binding, it's not difficult to sew into V's and pivot. Binding is best finished by hand. Draped over the side of a bed, a Scallop Border adds a final charming touch.

Pieced by Teresa Varnes
Quilted by Amie Potter
36" x 42"

Preparing Your Template

1. Find template pattern on page 229 in back of book and photocopy. A heavy acrylic ruler is available from Quilt in a Day for your purchase.

2. Glue photocopy to template plastic with glue stick, and cut out.

3. The bottom arc is for marking Scallops in lengths of 5" to 9". Use the smaller lengths as 5" to 7" for the Scallop pillow sham and small quilts, and lengths as 8" to 9" for larger quilts. Scallop instructions begin on page 201.

4. The top edge is for marking Waves or Vines in lengths of 4" to 9". Wave instructions begin on next page.

Lines represent breaks between Waves or Scallops.

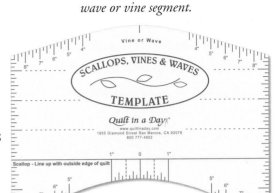

Each drawn curve is a wave or vine segment.

Each drawn arc is a scallop.

This Wave example shows five waves at top and bottom approximately 6" long. The five waves on the sides are approximately 8" long.

This Scallop example shows four scallops at top and bottom approximately 8" long. The five scallops on the sides are approximately 7½" long.

Making Waved Edge

Determining Number and Size of Waves

1. Draw lines on corners of outside Border using a hera marker or chalk marker. A hera marker makes a crease that does not have to be removed. Blue lines on the illustration represent marked lines.

2. Measure length and width minus corners, and record measurements.

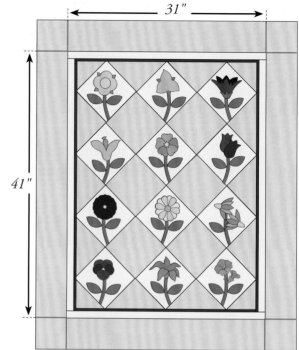

These sample measurements are from a lap quilt. Divide by odd numbers of 3 or 5 to find size of Waves.

3. Divide both measurements by an odd number as 3 or 5 for small quilts, and 7 or 9 for larger quilts. These odd numbers represent the number of Waves per side.

4. Select the same size Wave or two Waves that are closest in measurement for both length and width.

Example Width 31" x Length 41"

- Recalling multiplication tables may help you. Think of 31 as 5 x 6= 30 and 5 x 8 = 40. That leaves 1" for adjustment.
- The odd number is the number of waves.
- Length divided by number of waves = size of waves.
- 31" ÷ 5 is 6.2" (Five waves at 6"+)
- 41" ÷ 5 is 8.2" (Five waves at 8"+)

5. Mark centers of four sides of quilt top. Mark Border fabric with hera marker or chalk 1" in from outside edge. Use this guide line when marking Waves.

6. As a quick check, mark off selected measurements with chalk and a regular ruler.

Draw 1" guidelines for Waves less than 9", and guide lines 1½" in for 9" waves.

7. Place Glow-Line™ tape on template's selected measurements. As an extra check, measure the distance between the two marks with a regular ruler.

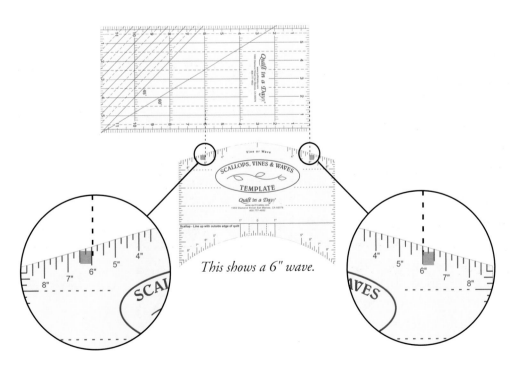

This shows a 6" wave.

Marking Waves

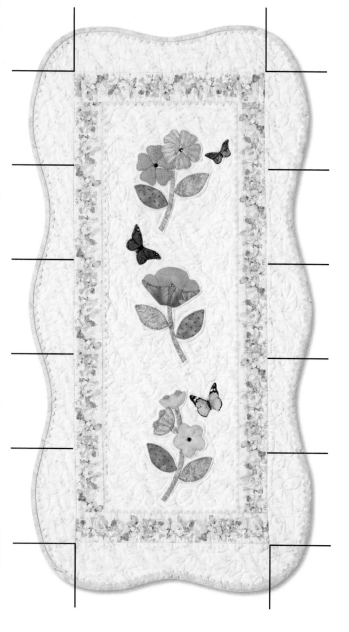

You can control the way the corners look on your quilt just by the way you mark the Waves. The direction of the Waves on each side of the corner must be the same.

Rounded Corners

On this example, Waves on both sides of corners turn out. Corners are nicely curved, making it easy to apply binding. Notice that the Wave on top and bottom centers turns in, and center wave on sides turns out.

Pieced by Patricia Knoechel
Quilted by Amie Potter
21" x 39"

Pointed Corners

On this example, Waves on both sides of corners turn in. Pointed corners are attractive but a bit more challenging to bind in comparison to rounded corners. Notice that the Wave on top and bottom centers turns out and center wave on sides turns in.

Pieced by Sue Bouchard
Quilted by Amie Potter
19" x 32"

1. Start on the top edge by placing Wave template on corner line with shape of Wave either in or out depending on shape of corner you selected. Line up selected size of Wave on guide line.

2. Trace length of Wave with hera marker or chalk. Put marks on ends.

This ruler is positioned toward edge of quilt to make a rounded corner.

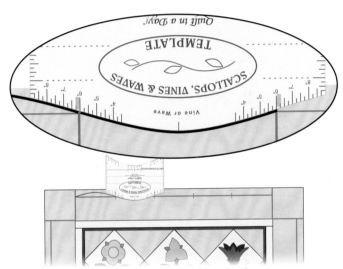

3. Turn template around with shape of wave going in opposite direction toward center of quilt. Place measurement on guide line, and match with marks. Trace Wave.

The direction of the wave on each side of the corner must be the same.

4. Prepare template for side Waves. Continue marking Waves from corner to center markings, alternating the direction of the Wave. You may need to elongate or shorten the center Waves.

If you prefer, practice marking waves on a strip of calculator tape cut the length and width minus corners.

Five 8" Scallops marked on 41" width

Five 6" Scallops marked on 31" width

199

Marking Corners

1. Cut a square piece of paper the size of the Border. Place square in corner, and mark ends of waves.

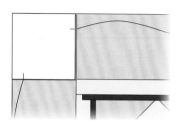

2. Fold paper on diagonal. Cut curve from mark to mark.

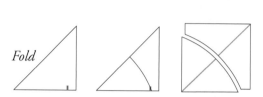

3. Use paper for template. Trace lines for corners. Smooth if necessary.

Finishing Wave

1. As a guide that will not be erased with handling, stitch on line with a long stitch length as 3.5 on computerized machine.

2. Layer quilt top with backing and batting. Quilt as desired. Stitch on Wave line through all thicknesses.

3. Waves may be trimmed ⅛" away from permanent guide line before adding bias binding or after adding bias binding.

4. **Bias Binding** begins on page 210.

Making Scalloped Edge

Determining Number and Size of Scallops

1. Measure width of top from corner to corner. Subtract 4" from total width. Record measurement.

2. Measure length of top from corner to corner and subtract 4" from total. Record measurement.

3. With a calculator, divide those measurements by 7", 8", or 9" to find the number of scallops per side.

4. If possible, select the same size scallop for both the length and width. Otherwise, select two that are close in size.

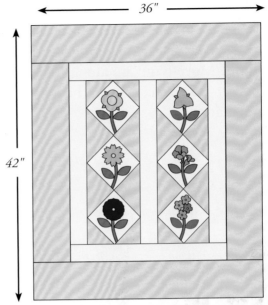

Five 7½" Scallops marked on 38" length

Four 8" Scallops marked on 32" width

The example is 36" x 42"

Subtract 4"   - 4"   - 4"

     32"   38"

Think of a number that can easily divide into both.
Eight is a good choice if you round 38" up to 40".

32 divided by 8 = 4
This is a simple easy number. You could make four 8" scallops.

38 divided by 8 is not as simple, but 40 divided by 8 = 5 is easy.

You could make five scallops just 7½", subtracting about ½" from 8" each time to make a 2" adjustment.

Marking Scallops

1. Mark diagonal lines with hera marker or chalk on four corners of quilt.

2. As a quick check, mark off selected measurements with chalk and a regular ruler across width of quilt. Move template along marks between corners to check. Check the length in the same manner.

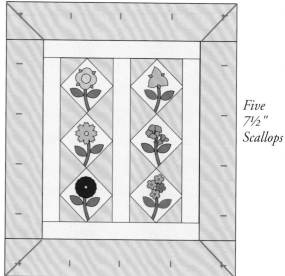

Five 7½" Scallops

Four 8" Scallops on top and bottom

3. Place corner of Scallop template on diagonal line. Line up selected size of scallop on diagonal line, and outside edge of quilt with solid straight line on template.

4. Trace Scallop with hera marker or chalk in case lines need to be removed. Mark Scallops from ends toward middle. If necessary, make adjustment in very center Scallop or Scallops to fit. You may need to elongate or shorten center Scallop.

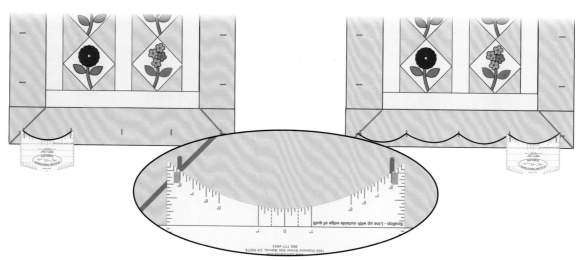

Template taped for 8" Scallop. Measure the distance between the two marks with a regular ruler.

5. Round corners outward.

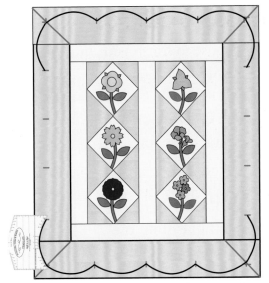

To mark a 7½" Scallop, add ¼" on each side of 7" marks.

6. As a permanent guide, topstitch on line with a long stitch length as 3.5 on computerized machine.

7. Layer quilt top with backing and batting. Quilt as desired inside scallop lines.

8. Scallops may be trimmed ⅛" away from permanent guide line before adding bias binding or after adding bias binding.

9. Bias Binding begins on page 210.

Planning Your Quilting

You May choose to finish your quilt one of these ways.

- Long Arm Quilting, page 205.
- Machine Quilting on a Conventional Sewing Machine, page 206.

Hand Quilting

1. In this antique quilt, the flowers were echo quilted ¼" away. Plain Background rows were then quilted with a grid 2" apart.

2. In this second antique quilt, plain Background rows were hand quilted with a Vine and Leaves. Diagonal grid lines fill in the rows.

3. The outside Border was quilted with Flowers and connecting Vines and Leaves.

Long Arm Quilting

Some quilters prefer to complete a top and send it to a long arm quilter. Follow these instructions if longarm quilting is your choice.

1. Clip loose threads.

2. Make sure there are no loose or unsewn seams.

3. Have top free of embellishments.

4. Press top and have it as wrinkle-free as possible. This applies to the backing fabric also.

5. The side measurements should be the same, and the top and bottom measurements should also be the same.

6. The backing fabric should be 4-6" longer and wider than the quilt top measurements. For example, if the quilt top is 90" x 108", then the backing should be 94" x 112" minimum.

7. The batting should be no less than 6" longer and wider than the pieced top measurements.

8. Do not pin the three layers together.

Pieced by Teresa Varnes
Long Arm Quilted by Carol Selepec

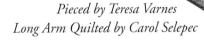

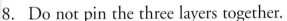

Some long arm quilters charge hourly prices depending on the density of the design, thread requests, and other factors. Others base the charge on the square inch size of the quilt. You local quilt shop can often provide the names of local long arm quilters if you need help locating one.

Layering Your Quilt

Follow these steps if you plan to quilt on a conventional sewing machine.

1. If necessary, piece Backing approximately 4"-6" larger than finished top.

2. Spread out Backing on a large table or floor area, right side down. Clamp fabric to edge of table with quilt clips, or tape Backing to the floor. Do not stretch Backing.

3. Layer Batting on Backing, also 4"-6" larger than finished top. Pat flat.

4. With right side up, center quilt on Batting and Backing. Smooth until all layers are flat. Clamp or tape outside edges.

Marking Diagonal Grid Lines

1. Place layered quilt flat on table.

2. Decide where to place grid lines. In this example, diagonal lines are marked in Background rows ¼" from edge of flowers.

3. Place 6" x 24" ruler's 45° line on seam line in selected area. Mark diagonal line with hera marker by pressing marker along side of ruler. A hera marker creases the fabric, marking it temporarily.

4. Move ruler 1½" to 2", or desired width of grid, lining up ruler's line with previous marked line. Mark again. Continue marking until area to be quilted is covered.

5. Turn ruler, and mark grid in opposite direction.

Quilting with Walking Foot and Guide

You can also place a quilting guide on your walking foot, and save time marking.

1. Draw one line, and quilt on that line with the walking foot.

2. Snap quilting guide down into groove on back of walking foot. Set guide to desired width of grid.

3. Place guide on stitched line, and stitch again.

4. Continue quilting until area is covered.

Safety Pinning

1. Place pin covers on 1" safety pins with needle nose pliers.

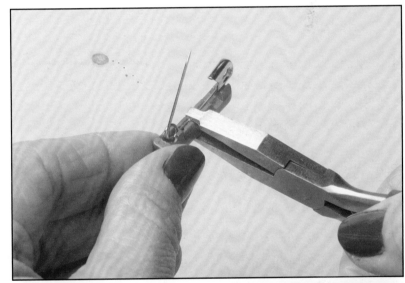

2. Pin away from where you plan to quilt. Catch tip of pin in grooves on pinning tool, and close pins.

3. Safety pin through all layers three to five inches apart.

4. Use pinning tool to open pins when removing them. Store pins opened.

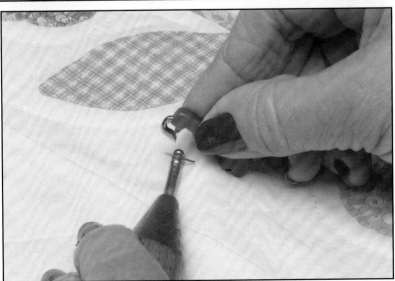

Echo Quilting Around Flowers with a Darning Foot

1. Attach darning foot to sewing machine. Drop feed dogs or cover feed dogs with a plate. No stitch length is required as you control the length. Use a fine needle and matching thread in the top and in the bobbin. Use needle down position.

2. Place hands flat along row of Flowers to be echo quilted. Bring bobbin thread up ¼" on seam line or edge of design.

3. Lock stitch and clip thread tails.

4. Using edge of darning foot as a grid, continuously quilt ¼" away from edge of flowers.

5. Sew down one side of the Flowers, turn, and echo quilt second side.

Thread your machine with matching thread and quilt ¼" away for echo quilting.

Quilting on Grid Lines

1. Thread your machine with matching thread. Match the bobbin thread to top thread to eliminate chance of bobbin thread showing on top surface.

2. Attach your walking foot, and lengthen the stitch to 8 to 10 stitches per inch or 3.0 to 3.5 on a computerized machine.

3. Roll quilt on diagonal. Place hands on quilt in triangular shape. Quilt on grid lines, locking beginning and ending stitches.

4. "Stitch in the ditch" around Borders.

Thread your machine with matching thread and quilt on grid lines with long stitches.

Bias and Straight Cut Bindings

Making Bias Binding for Curved Outside Edges

1. Cut Binding fabric into 16" selvage to selvage strips so ruler can reach from edge to edge.

2. Line up 45° line on 6" x 24" ruler with left edge of 16" strip.

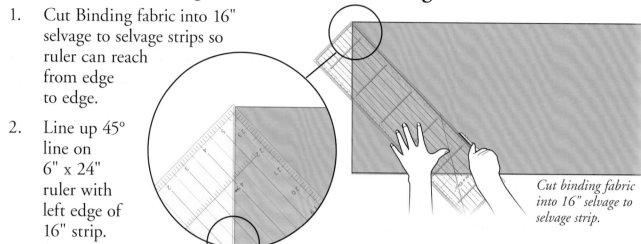

Cut binding fabric into 16" selvage to selvage strip.

45° angle

3. Cut on diagonal. Fabric from triangle to left of ruler can be cut into bias strips as well.

4. Move ruler over 2¼" from diagonal cut. Cut again.

5. Cut 16" strip into as many 2¼" bias strips as needed for your size quilt.

   Experienced quilters often prefer using 2" bias strips.

6. Piece bias strips together on an angle to outside measurements of your quilt.

   Rainbow bias strips are pieced together in same manner.

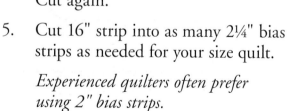

Putting Glow Line™ tape on 2¼" line helps to locate cutting measurement quickly.

⅜" tip

⅜" tip

210

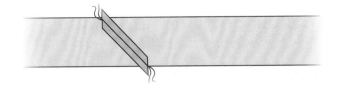

7. Press diagonal seams open.

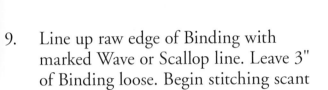

8. Press bias strip in half lengthwise wrong sides together.

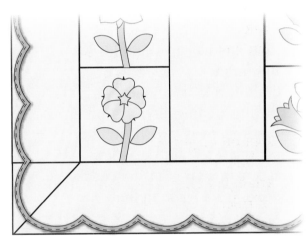

9. Line up raw edge of Binding with marked Wave or Scallop line. Leave 3" of Binding loose. Begin stitching scant ¼" seam in middle of line.

   Scallop: Stitch to point between two Scallops. Stop with needle in fabric. Raise presser foot, pivot and continue stitching around quilt.

10. **Ease Binding** around curves. Do not stretch Binding.

Waves or Scallops may be turned ⅛" away from permanent guide line before adding bias binding or after adding bias binding.

11. Stop stitching 4" from where ends will overlap and straight cuts.

12. Line up the two ends of Binding. Trim excess with a ½" overlap and straight cuts.

13. Open up folded ends and pin right sides together. Sew a ¼" seam.

14. Continue stitching Binding in place.

15. Trim quilt top even with Binding. Clip between Scallops to seam.

16. **Turn Binding** to back side. Pull folded edge over stitching line. Inside corners will automatically fold in place. Hand stitch folded edge.

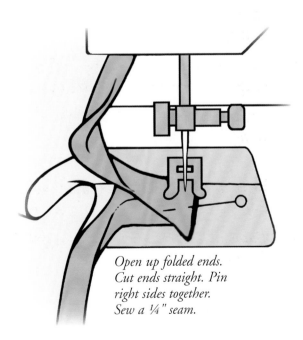

Open up folded ends. Cut ends straight. Pin right sides together. Sew a ¼" seam.

211

Making Straight Cut Binding

These instructions show how to make a one-fabric Binding. If desired, make a Rainbow Binding by cutting leftover Flower fabric into 3" wide strips by any length and piece them together to fit around outside edge of quilt top. Follow these instructions for either one.

1. Square off selvage edges, and sew 3" Binding strips together lengthwise. Fold and press in half with wrong sides together.

2. Place walking foot attachment on sewing machine and regular thread on top and in bobbin to match Binding.

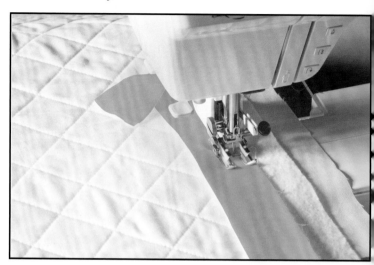

3. Line up raw edges of folded Binding with raw edges of quilt in middle of one side. Begin stitching 4" from end of Binding. Sew with 10 stitches per inch, or 3.0 to 3.5. Sew approximately ⅜" from edge, or width of walking foot.

4. Place pin ⅜" from corner.

5. At corner, stop stitching by pin ⅜" in from edge with needle in fabric. Remove pin. Raise presser foot and turn quilt toward corner.

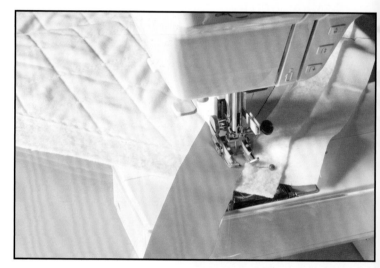

6. Put presser foot down. Stitch diagonally off edge of Binding.

7. Raise foot, and pull quilt forward slightly.

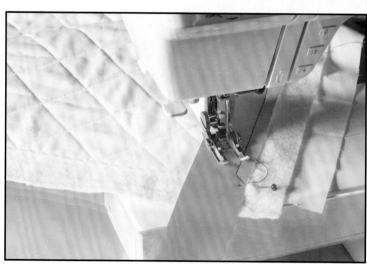

8. Turn quilt to next side.

9. Fold Binding strip straight up on diagonal. Fingerpress diagonal fold.

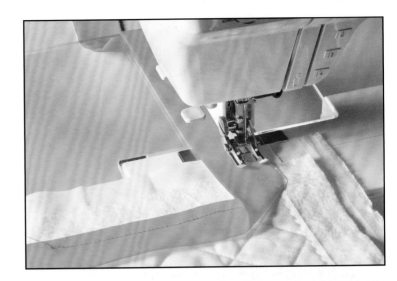

10. Fold Binding strip straight down with diagonal fold underneath. Line up top of fold with raw edge of Binding underneath.

11. Begin sewing from edge.

12. Continue stitching and mitering corners around outside of quilt.

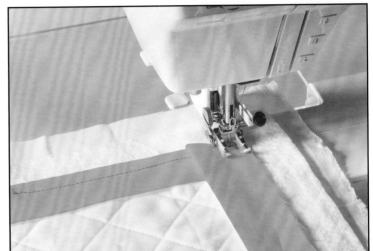

13. Stop stitching 4" from where ends will overlap.

14. Line up two ends of Binding. Trim excess with ½" overlap.

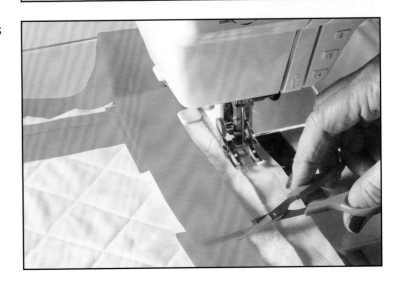

15. Open out folded ends and pin right sides together. Sew a ¼" seam. Press seam open.

16. Continue stitching Binding in place.

17. Trim Batting and Backing up to ⅛" from raw edges of Binding.

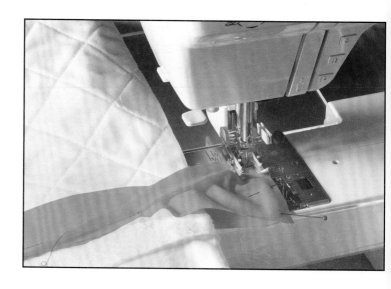

18. Fold back Binding.

19. Pull Binding to back side of quilt. Pin in place so that folded edge on Binding covers stitching line. Tuck in excess fabric at each miter on diagonal.

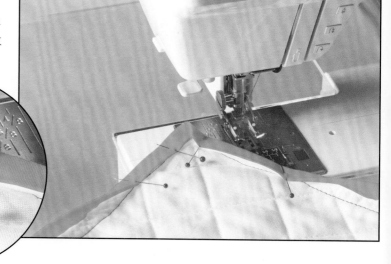

20. From right side, "stitch in the ditch" using invisible or matching thread on front side, and bobbin thread to match Binding on back side. Catch folded edge of Binding on the back side with stitching.

    Optional: Hand stitch Binding in place.

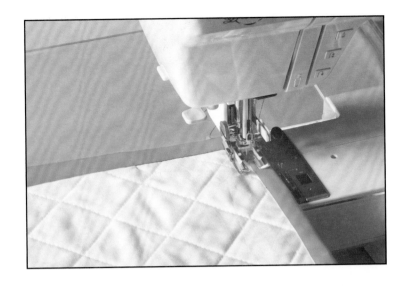

21. Hand stitch miter.

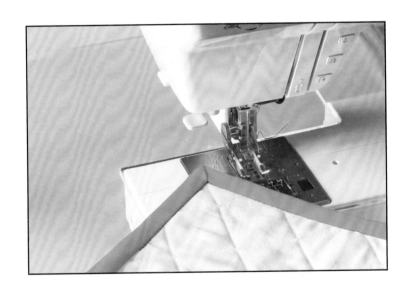

22. Sew identification label on Back.

    - name of maker
    - place where quilt was made
    - year
    - name of quilt
    - any other pertinent information.

Embellishing with Crystals

Hot Fix crystals or rhinestones are a great way of embellishing your quilt after it has been quilted and bound. The quilt can be machine washed and dried using gentle, cool settings. Recommended sizes are 4mm and 5mm Swarovski® Crystals.

1. The hot fix tools use a variety of tips. Place a tip the size of your crystal on your tool before you plug it in. It is too hot to touch once it's turned on.

2. Using tweezers, position crystal on quilt.

3. Holding crystal in place, use hot applicator wand to activate glue on back of crystal. Keep hot applicator in place for 8 to 10 seconds.

Hold hot applicator in place for 8 to 10 seconds.

4. Check to make sure crystals are in place. If loose, repeat process.

Crystals can be machine washed and dried.

Hot fix crystals were positioned on the quilt to enhance the quilting designs.

Pieced by Sue Bouchard
Quilted by Amie Potter
41" x 50"

Pillow Sham

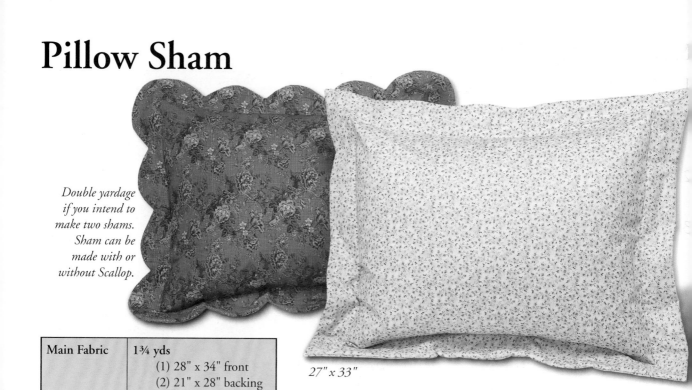

Double yardage if you intend to make two shams. Sham can be made with or without Scallop.

27" x 33"

Main Fabric	1¾ yds
	(1) 28" x 34" front
	(2) 21" x 28" backing
Batting	1 yd
	(1) 28" x 34"

Making Sham

1. Hem one 28" side on both backing pieces.

2. Place backing pieces right sides together to front piece, overlapping hems in center. Match outside edges.

3. Place on top of batting with backing wrong side up. Pin.

4. For straight edge, sew ¼" seam around outside edge.

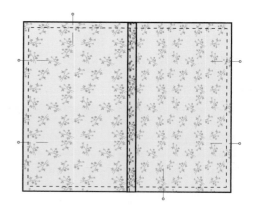

Making Scallop Edge

1. Find template pattern on page 229 in back of book and photocopy. A heavy acrylic ruler is available from Quilt in a Day for your purchase.

2. Glue photocopy to template plastic with glue stick, and cut out.

3. The bottom arc is for marking Scallops in lengths of 5" to 9". Use the 6" length for the Scallop pillow sham.

4. Draw 45° lines on four corners of backing piece.

5. Place corner of Scallop template on diagonal line. Line up 6" line on template with diagonal line. Trace inside of Scallop with marking pen from 6" mark to 6" mark.

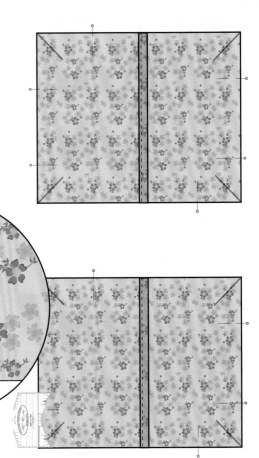

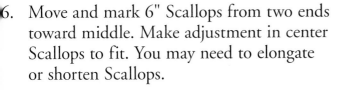

6. Move and mark 6" Scallops from two ends toward middle. Make adjustment in center Scallops to fit. You may need to elongate or shorten Scallops.

7. Sew on Scallop line. Trim ¼" away from stitched line, and clip curves.

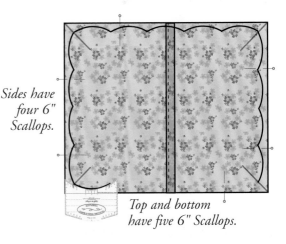

Sides have four 6" Scallops.

Top and bottom have five 6" Scallops.

Finishing Sham

1. Turn right side out.

2. Mark stitching line 3" from straight outside edge, or 3" from top of Scallop.

3. Quilt on line.

4. Stuff with standard size pillow.

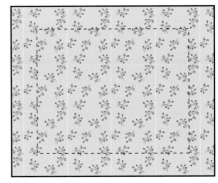

Three Flower Wallhanging

Choose your favorite Flowers for this small wallhanging. The Flowers are appliquéd on crisp white background with side and corner triangles and blocks are set on point.

1. Sew and turn parts of three selected Flowers. Make a total of six Leaves. Sew blocks and set aside.

2. Cut one 11½" square on both diagonals for Side Triangles.

3. Cut two 6½" squares on one diagonal for Corners.

4. Lay out pieces in vertical row and sew together following directions beginning on page 170.

5. Straighten outside edges, leaving ¼" seam allowance.

6. Sew rickrack to outside edge.

7. Sew on Border. Quilt and bind.

*Appliquéed and Pieced
by Patricia Knoechel
Quilted by Amie Potter
18" x 36"*

Yardage Chart

Background	⅝ yd (1) 11½" square for Side Triangles (3) 7½" squares for Flower Blocks (2) 6½" squares for Corners
Three Flowers of Your Choice	Follow each Flower for yardage requirements.
Fusible Interfacing	¼ yd
Stems and Leaves	¼ yd Cut into (3) 1¼" x 7" bias strips for Stems (3) 3½" x 4" for Leaves
Border	½ yd (4) 4" strips
Rickrack	1½ yds of ¾" wide rickrack
Backing	⅔ yd
Batting	24" x 40"
Binding	⅓ yd (3) 2¾" strips

Five Flower Wallhanging

This small project is an easy way to make a continuous Vine on one long strip without cutting individual 7½" Background squares for Flowers.

Supplies

Hera marker or chalk
> Hera marker makes a crease line that does not have to be removed as a pencil mark.

Scallop, Vine, and Wave Template
> Paper template provided on page 229. Template is available on heavy acrylic from Quilt in a Day.

9½" Square Up Ruler
¼" Foot
Appliqué Foot
Straw and Bodkin
Stilleto
Wooden Iron
Small Sharp Scissors

Pieced by Patricia Knoechel
Quilted by Amie Potter
19" x 45"

Yardage Chart

Background	1 yd (1) 7 ½" x 42" for Center piece (3) 3" strips for First Border (3) 4 ½" strips for Second Border
Five Flowers of Your Choice	Follow each Flower for yardage requirements.
Light weight Non-woven Fusible Interfacing	½ yd Quick Turn Appliqué is preferred so you don't see outline of Vine underneath Flowers.
Green Vine	¼ yd (3) 1 ¼" x 12" bias strips for Vine (1) 3 ½" x 25" strip for Leaves
½" Rickrack	3 pkgs
Backing	1½ yds
Batting	25" x 51"
Bias Binding	½ yd (1) 16" piece Cut into (8) 2¼" bias strips

Making the Flowers

1. Select your five favorite Flowers.

2. Sew and turn Flower parts. Make a total of eleven Leaves. Set aside.

Marking the Background

1. Trim selvages.

2. Start at left end of 7½" Background strip. With hera marker or chalk and 9½" Square up Ruler, mark a seam line ¼" from edge.

3. Mark line 7" from seam line. Continue marking lines every 7" for a total of five 7" squares.

4. Add a ¼" seam line at right, and trim off excess fabric.

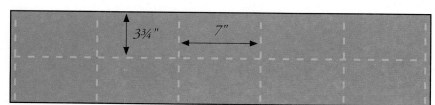

5. Mark guide line at 3¾". The guide line

Dotted lines represent crease lines.

is used in marking the Vine, and will be invisible in the finished Wallhanging.

Marking the Vine

1. Start with first square on left end. Position Vine template, matching 7" marks on ruler with marked square and guide line. Draw line along top of template from 7" to 7".

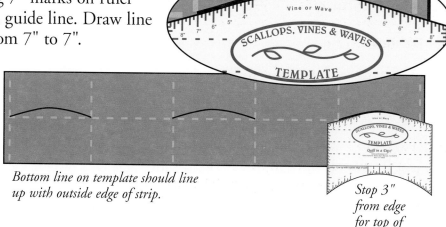

2. Skip second square. Slide template to third square. Mark Vine, repeating step #1.

3. Skip fourth square. Slide template to fifth square. Mark Vine, stopping 3" from edge for top of Vine.

Bottom line on template should line up with outside edge of strip.

Stop 3" from edge for top of Vine.

4. Turn strip around. Mark second and fourth squares with Vine in alternating direction. Connect lines from one square to the next, creating a continuous Vine.

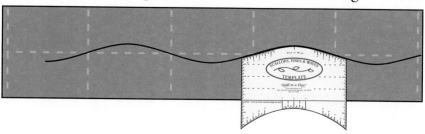

Sewing the Vine

1. Piece together three 1¼" green bias strips to 36" length. Press seams open.

2. Press strip in half lengthwise with wrong sides together.

3. Start with bottom block. Place raw edges of folded bias strip on inside curve of line. Sew with scant ¼" seam. To make a scant ¼", move ¼" needle position slightly to right.

4. Start sewing on right block and stop 3" from end. Trim excess Vine.

5. Fold bias strip back over raw edge and press flat. Stem should cover raw edge.

6. Sew folded edge to Background by hand or machine. See page 40.

Stop Vine 3" from end of block.

Start here.

Adding Flowers and Leaves

1. Using the 7" marked lines as a guide, place tops of Flowers on each square ½" below line.

2. Arrange two Leaves below each Flower. Check for even spacing between Flowers and Leaves.

3. Tuck top Leaf under top Flower and pin in place. Leave top edge of Leaf open, and fuse after First Border is in place.

4. Fuse Flowers and Leaves in place. Hand or machine sew outside edges. For machine sewing, roll ends of strip toward center for ease in sewing.

5. Fuse bottom Leaf in place after First Border is added.

6. Embellish centers of Flowers.

Tuck top Leaf under top Flower. Leave top edge of Leaf open, and fuse after First Border is in place.

Adding First and Second Borders

1. Sew 3" First Border strips to two long sides. Press seams toward Border, and square corners.

2. Sew 3" First Border strips to top and bottom. Press seams toward Border, and square corners.

3. Line up edge of ½" rickrack with raw edges of top.

4. With less than ¼" seam, sew rickrack around outside edges of First Border. Lengthen stitch to avoid puckers.

5. Sew 4½" Second Border strips to two long sides, press seams toward Border and square corners.

6. Sew 4½" strips to top and bottom, press seams toward Border and square corners.

Marking Wavy Outside Edges

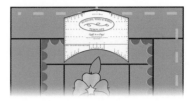

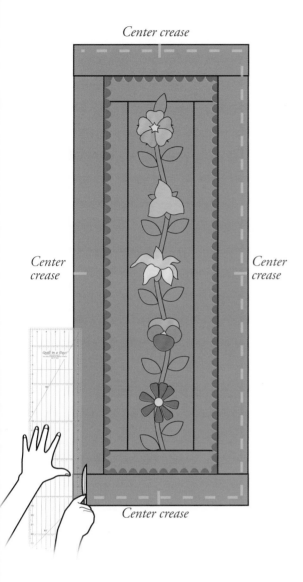

Center crease

Center crease

Center crease

Center crease

3. Place template with dotted line on seam, and 4" Wave line on guide line. Center lines on ruler and fabric should line up.

4. Draw Wave line from 4" to 4". Mark ends.

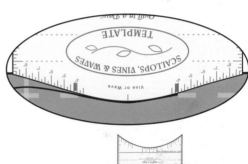

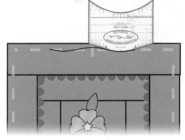

1. Fold sides in half, and crease centers.

2. With hera marker or chalk and 6" x 24" Ruler, draw guide line on Second Border 1" from outside edge on four sides.

5. Turn template. Connect second 4" Wave in alternating direction on guide line, and draw Wave. Mark ends.

6. Connect and draw third 4" Wave on other side of center.

7. Mark opposite end of Wallhanging with 4" Waves.

Marking Corners

1. Trace Corner template on template plastic, and cut out.

2. Line up Corner template on each corner, and trace outside edge.

Marking 5½" Waves on Side Borders

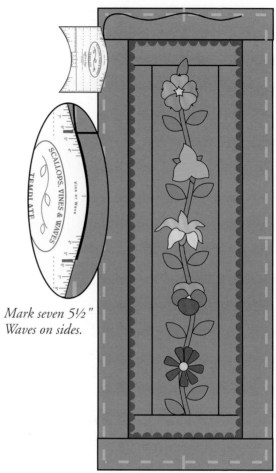

Mark seven 5½" Waves on sides.

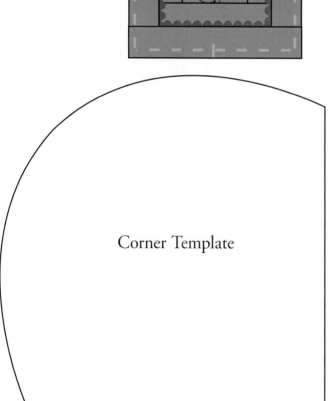

Corner Template

1. Start at corner. Line up dotted ruler line with Border's outside edge. To get a 5½" Wave, add ¼" on each side of 5" Wave. Draw 5½" Wave on guide line.

2. Turn template in alternating direction, and draw a connecting 5½" Wave on guide line.

3. Mark opposite end of same side.

Finishing the Wallhanging

1. Layer and quilt. Follow directions beginning on pages 206.

2. Stitch on marked Wave line.

3. Line up peaks of rickrack on Wave line, and stitch with less than ¼" seam. See rickrack on Wallhanging on page 221.

4. Sew bias binding to outside edge. Follow directions beginning on page 210.

Dash lines indicate where Wave breaks.

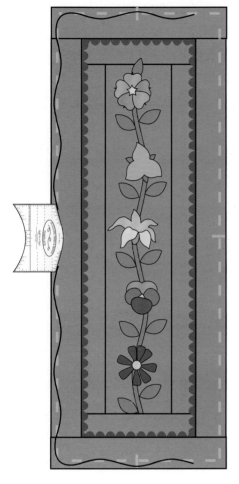

4. Continue alternating direction of template and drawing connecting Waves.

5. On the final center Wave, make a length adjustment. It may be slightly larger.

Teresa did not trim her center piece, so she had fabric to place six Flowers on her Wallhanging.

Pieced by Teresa Varnes
Quilted by Janna Mitchell
18" x 52"

Preparing for Spring

To turn the mind from winter weather, Linda used the Magic Vine flowers to make her quilt a display of flower seed packs. Each flower is appliquéd with the raw edge technique and finished with coordinating thread in a machine blanket stitch. The cream background fabric was also used for the lattice and cornerstones. The flower names were created on a computer and copied to photo transfer fabric. A simple black binding was added as the finishing touch.

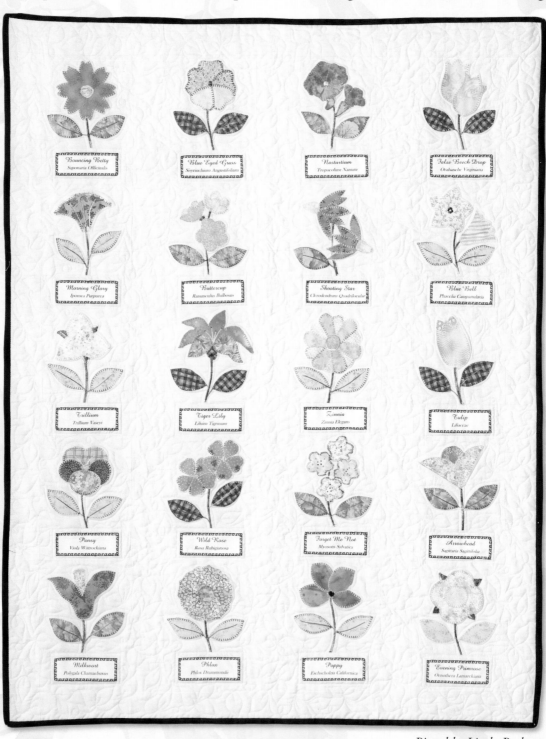

Pieced by Linda Parker
Quilted by Amie Potter
40" x 51"

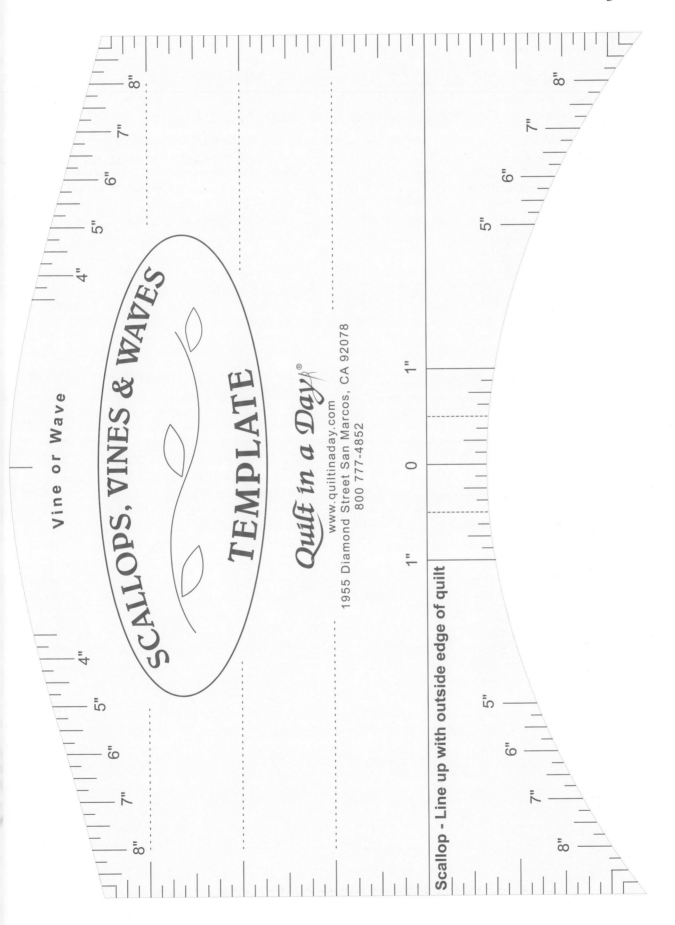

Vine or Wave

SCALLOPS, VINES & WAVES

TEMPLATE

Quilt in a Day®
www.quiltinaday.com
1955 Diamond Street San Marcos, CA 92078
800 777-4852

Scallop - Line up with outside edge of quilt

Index

More Appliqué Books by Quilt in a Day

Quilt in a Day books offer a wide range of techniques and are directed toward a variety of skill levels. If you do not have a quilt shop in your area, you may write or call for a complete catalog and current price list of all books and patterns published by Quilt in a Day®, Inc.

Grandmother's Garden Quilt, based on Florence LaGanke's Nancy Page Quilt Club of the late 1920's. Full size patterns and placement guides included. **$27.95**

Printed Fusible Interfacing plus templates are also available. **$18.95** per package for 20 flowers

Applique in a Day, based on the Baltimore Album Quilt, teaches a quick and easy method of making applique fun. Features 12 different blocks and two border treatments. **$24.95**

Three different fusible interfacing packages are available.
$18.95 per package
12 Blocks
Scallop Border
Floral Border

Garden Lattice Quilts combine traditional piecing to make lattice, and applique to grow flowers with either fussy cut single flowers or clusters. Step-by-step directions with full color illustrations. **$14.95**

One of the best loved of all traditional patterns, *Sunbonnet Sue visits Quilt in a Day* for quick and easy applique techniques. Complete yardage and cutting charts included.
$10.95
Printed Fusible Interfacing for Sue and Sam is also available.
$6.95 per package

New for Magic Vine!
Printed Non-Woven Fusible Interfacing with 22 Flowers and Leaves for Quick Turn Appliqué.

Printed Paper Backed Fusible Web with 22 Flowers and Leaves for Raw Edge Appliqué.

Quilt in a Day®, Inc. • 1955 Diamond Street • San Marcos, CA 92078
800 777-4852 • Fax: 760 591-4424 • www.quiltinaday.com

231

With her mind on spring, Patricia selected three flowers for her wallhanging in cheerful pastels and set her blocks on point with side triangles. She used quick-turn appliqué for the flowers and finished them with the blanket stitch. Her flowers are embellished with embroidery thread, buttons, and a stone bead. With jumbo rick-rack, Patricia framed her blocks and followed up with a soft yellow border print with mitered corners. She echoed the frame with green binding. For a charming finish, Amie quilted vines, leaves and flowers in the borders and used a small stencil for depth in the side and corner triangles.

Appliquéd and Pieced by Patricia Knoechel
Machine Quilted by Amie Potter
18" x 36"